WOMEN, TRAINING AND THE SKILLS SHORTAGE
THE CASE FOR PUBLIC INVESTMENT

The Policy Studies Institute (PSI) is Britain's leading independent research organisation undertaking studies of economic, industrial and social policy, and the workings of political institutions.

PSI is a registered charity, run on a non-profit basis, and is not associated with any political party, pressure group or commercial interest.

PSI attaches great importance to covering a wide range of subject areas with its multi-disciplinary approach. The Institute's 30+ researchers are organised in teams which currently cover the following programmes:

Family Finances
Health Studies and Social Care
Innovation and New Technology
Quality of Life and the Environment
Social Justice and Social Order
Employment Studies
Arts and the Cultural Industries
Information Policy
Education

This publication arises from the Employment Studies programme and is one of over 30 publications made available by the Institute each year.

Information about the work of PSI, and a catalogue of available books can be obtained from:

Marketing Department, PSI
100 Park Village East, London NW1 3SR

WOMEN, TRAINING AND THE SKILLS SHORTAGE

THE CASE FOR PUBLIC INVESTMENT

Joan Payne

POLICY **S**TUDIES **I**NSTITUTE
100 PARK VILLAGE EAST, LONDON NW1 3SR
Tel: 071-387 2171 Fax: 071-388 0914

The publishing imprint of the independent
POLICY STUDIES INSTITUTE
100 Park Village East, London NW1 3SR
Telephone: 071-387 2171; Fax: 071-388 0914

PSI Report No 714

ISBN 0 85374 505 6

A CIP catalogue record of this book is available from the British Library.

1 2 3 4 5 6 7 8 9

How to obtain PSI publications
All book shop and individual orders should be sent to PSI's distributors:
BEBC Ltd
9 Albion Close, Parkstone, Poole, Dorset, BH12 3LL

Books will normally be despatched in 24 hours. Cheques should be made payable to BEBC Ltd.

Credit card and telephone/fax orders may be placed on the following freephone numbers:
FREEPHONE: 0800 262260 FREEFAX: 0800 262266

Booktrade Representation (UK & Eire)
Book Representation Ltd
P O Box 17, Canvey Island, Essex SS8 8HZ

PSI Subscriptions
PSI Publications are available on subscription.
Further information from PSI's subscription agent:
Carfax Publishing Company Ltd
Abingdon Science Park, P O Box 25, Abingdon OX14 3UE

Laserset by Policy Studies Institute
Printed in Great Britain by Billing & Sons Ltd, Worcester

To the memory of my Father

Contents

Page

Preface

1 Training policy and women 1

2 Women's need for training 24

3 The training experience 40

4 Segregation in training 53

5 Finding work 69

6 Training and career change 96

7 Earnings 110

8 The difference training makes 126

9 Summary and conclusions:
the case for public investment 142

Appendix 1: Survey methods 160

Appendix 2: Statistical models 168

References 187

Tables

Page

1.1 Women as a percentage of all workers by occupation, 1971 to 1995   6

1.2 Occupations of men and women with the same qualifications, GB 1987/88   7

2.1 Qualifications of women trainees on TOPS/OJTS compared with the qualifications of all women in GB who were in work or unemployed in 1986, by age   35

3.1 Training field of TOPS/OJTS trainees, by sex   42

3.2 Training occupations of trainees on Employment Training, by sex, 1989/90   44

3.3 Comparison between the qualifications gained by TOPS/OJTS trainees and trainees on Employment Training   49

4.1 Ethnic balance in training fields on TOPS/OJTS, by sex   64

4.2 Skill level of TOPS/OJTS course, by ethnic origin and sex   65

5.1 Women's movements between full-time and part-time work before and after training   84

5.2 Placement rates on TOPS/OJTS compared with Employment Training   88

6.1 Changes in the occupations of women trainees after training   98

6.2 Transition matrix for women trainees' last job before training and their first job afterwards   99

6.3 Changes in the industries in which women trainees were employed after training   108

6.4	Transition matrix for the industry of the last job before training and the first job afterwards: women	109
7.1	Mean earnings (uprated to October 1987 values) before and after training, by sex	112
7.2	Distribution of earnings gains and losses, by sex	114
7.3	Mean difference in earnings before and after training, by level of earnings before training	115
7.4	Earnings before and after training for different groups of women trainees	119
8.1	Earnings and career breaks: women trainees compared with members of the comparison sample	139

Figures

		Page
5.1	Proportion of TOPS/OJTS trainees in employment three months after completing training; quarterly, 1980-1988	72
5.2	Proportion of TOPS/OJTS trainees in employment three months after completing training, by sex; quarterly, 1979-1982	73
5.3	Proportion of TOPS/OJTS trainees in employment three months after completing training, by course type; quarterly, 1983-1988	75
5.4	Percentage of trainees in work over the ten months after the end of their course, by sex	78
5.5	Percentage of trainees in work using the skills in which they had trained over the ten months after the end of their course, by sex	80
5.6	Percentage of women trainees in work over the ten months after the end of their course, by the length of time since they had last worked before the start of their course	82
7.1	Distribution of gross hourly earnings before and after training, by sex	113
A1.1	Percentage of men in trainee and comparison samples who were unemployed in each month from January 1980 until interview	165
A1.2	Percentage of women in trainee and comparison samples who were in work in each month from January 1980 until interview	166

Models

		Page
1	Proportional hazards model for number of months before entry to the first job after the end of training	169
2	Proportional hazards model for number of months before entry to the first job after the end of training which used the skills learned	171
3	OLS regression model for the change in women's earnings after training	173
4	Logit model for employment in the period April 1987 - September 1987: combined trainee and comparison sample, women	175
5	Logit model for employment in the period April 1987 - September 1987: combined trainee and comparison sample, men	177
6	Logit model for job satisfaction in current job: combined trainee and comparison sample, women	179
7	Logit model for job satisfaction in current job: combined trainee and comparison sample, men	181
8	OLS regression model for earnings: combined trainee and control sample, women	183
9	OLS regression model for earnings: combined trainee and comparison sample, men	185

Preface

My interest in adult training began with my involvement in a research project funded by the Training Agency (now part of the Employment Department), the results of which were published last year (Payne, 1990). This research had many implications for training policy, and particularly for the training of women, which could not be brought out in the original technical report. The work of developing these implications has been funded by a grant from the Nuffield Foundation, for whose support I am most grateful. I would like to stress that all the opinions expressed in this book are entirely my own, and should in no way be attributed to either of the two organisations that have been involved in funding the work.

In writing a book such as this it is always difficult to strike the right balance between on the one hand giving enough technical detail to satisfy those with a more specialised interest in the field, and on the other, giving so much detail that the general reader loses interest. I have tried to achieve this balance, but if any readers feel that the detail is sometimes inadequate, either in the main text or in the appendices, they will probably find that the original research report gives the information required.

Many people were involved in one way or another in the original research project, and their contribution is acknowledged in the report which has already been published. The idea of developing the report into a book came from Michael White, for whose encouragement I am very grateful. The work has demanded considerable re-analysis of the original data, and I should like to thank Martin Range, whose programming skill has enabled me to use the data in ways that would not otherwise have been possible. Most of all I wish to thank the trainees for agreeing to take part, especially the many among them who took the trouble to write detailed accounts of their experience of training. Thanks are also due to members of the comparison sample, to whom the study had no obvious relevance, but who nevertheless gave their time to be interviewed.

1. Training Policy and Women

Britain wastes the talents and energies of many of her citizens. Some want to work and cannot; others work at a level far below their potential. Many able people lack the qualifications they need for advancement; others are trapped without work in towns whose industry has died. Older people are often forced into premature retirement; black people are frequently obstructed by racial prejudice. This book is about how women's contribution to the workforce can be developed so that their abilities are more fully used, but that does not mean that these other forms of waste are unimportant. In economic terms they all undermine the competitiveness of the nation; in personal terms they can all lead to frustration, poverty and unhappiness.

The book draws on a nationally based study which aimed to measure the impact of an adult vocational training programme on the lives of those who took part. This training was of high quality, and was available nationally under the Training Opportunities Programme TOPS, later renamed the Old Job Training Scheme. It was sometimes undertaken to update old skills, sometimes to upgrade existing skills, and sometimes to acquire skills in an entirely new field. The Evaluation Study assessed the contribution that this retraining made to the subsequent employment prospects, earnings and job satisfaction of trainees.

The Evaluation Study led to a number of important conclusions, relevant to both men and women. This book develops those that particularly relate to women, for whom adult training has a special role to play.

Two premises provide the starting point for the argument: first, that the British labour force does not possess in sufficient quantity the skills that are needed for the economy to compete in European and world markets; and second, that although women are an increasingly important part of Britain's workforce, their potential contribution is grossly under-valued and under-developed. A long-term solution to

1

Britain's skills problems will not be found without far-reaching reforms in the way in which we educate and train our young people. Even so, Britain could go a long way towards meeting her skills needs if she made better use of mature women workers.

The causes of women's under-achievement are deep-rooted and complex, and tackling them calls for action on many fronts. One of these is wider access to high quality adult training, and to achieve this there must be much greater public investment. The book will show how in personal terms access to training under TOPS/OJTS brought substantial benefits to women, and will also provide evidence that, in economic terms, public investment in women's training makes sound good sense. This is because adult training significantly increased both the amount of labour which women contributed to the economy and the skill level at which they worked. We begin, however, with the premisses of the argument.

The British skills gap
As soon as the British economy started to recover from the deep recession of the early 1980's, the press began to carry stories of skills shortages. Such shortages are a recurring feature of the industrial cycle in Britain. At times of reduced demand, one of the first steps that employers take to cut costs is to slim down their training programmes. The result is that when demand picks up, often there is insufficient skilled labour available to allow production to be built up again quickly enough to keep pace with demand. The outcome is a familiar one in Britain: imports are sucked in to fill the vacuum.

Today's skills shortages stem partly from this cyclical pattern, but there are other, more profound problems involved. Many people believe that the shortages are symptomatic of a basic mis-match between the skills needs of an advanced industrial economy and the capacity of Britain's system of vocational education to supply those needs. In the 1980's skills shortages, especially in the new technologies, existed side-by-side with massive unemployment, and the shortages are persisting even as the economy slides back into recession. The causes lie in fundamental changes in Britain's industrial base.

The British economy is finding less and less use for unskilled and unqualified workers. Technological change has automated many operations that used to be done by hand, and more than a million semi-skilled jobs for plant and machine operatives have disappeared in the UK since 1971, together with nearly half a million labouring jobs. But not only have machines replaced people; the industrial balance of the country has shifted. In 1975, at least three out of every ten jobs were in manufacturing industry; in 1995 less than two in ten will be. This means over two and a half million fewer jobs in manufacturing in the space of two decades. In 1975, business services and other marketed services gave employment to around one in eight workers. In 1995 nearly a quarter - three million more people - will earn their living in this way.[1]

During much of the last decade the consequences of all this change were to be seen in the dole queues, particularly the lengthy queues of old and poorly skilled workers who could find no place in the new Britain. It was only with the economic upturn towards the end of the decade that the other half of the story hit the headlines. Britain's employers started to report serious difficulties in recruiting skilled labour. A national survey in 1990 found that 22 per cent of employers in establishments with 25 or more employees were experiencing recruitment difficulties, and 17 per cent said that there was a significant gap between the skills of their workforce and those they needed to meet their business objectives. They saw the consequences as a brake on development, loss of business to competitors, and increased costs.[2]

The need for more highly skilled and qualified workers emerges on several fronts. The expansion of the service sector has meant that the number of jobs for professionals, semi- or associate professionals, managers and administrators has grown enormously, and will continue to grow. In 1995 there will be three and a quarter million more people employed at these levels than there were in 1971. These jobs need to be filled by people with good educational qualifications, and our education system has not kept pace. Official figures show that in 1986 only a third of 16 to 18 year olds in Britain were in full-time education or training, a much lower figure than for all our major competitors. The proportion is much higher in some European countries that we have been accustomed to regard as economically more backward than Britain, such as Italy, where the proportion is 47 per cent, and even Spain, where it is now 52 per cent.[3]

In manufacturing industry today productivity depends heavily on the ability to implement technological change quickly and efficiently.

A critical factor for success is the level of skill of the workforce which must accept and adapt to the new technologies, and this in turn depends on the strength of the system of vocational training. Here as well as in academic education Britain compares badly with her industrial competitors. Every year, for example, Germany trains about half as many more engineering students to degree standard or higher than does the UK, and the standard of the German degrees is higher than in Britain. The gap between the two countries is just as great in the training of engineering technicians, and in addition every year more than three times as many young people qualify at craft level in engineering in Germany than in the UK.[4] In other vocational fields the comparison between Britain and other leading industrial nations is equally unfavourable.

It is clear, then, that unless there are big improvements in the skill level of Britain's labour force, more and more ground will be lost to our industrial competitors. It is natural to look to the next generation to supply these skills, and the case for much greater investment in young people's education and training is overwhelming. But there is a lot of ground to be made up, and in the meantime our competitors are planning to increase their own investment at a faster rate than we in this country appear to be willing to envisage. While Britain prevaricates, the competition is pulling away. Even with a substantial improvement now, it will be some years before we reap the harvest of skills among future generations. In the meantime the demographic timebomb continues to tick. The number of people in Britain aged between 16 and 19 has been falling for some years, and will reach its nadir in 1994. In the space of a decade their numbers will have fallen by more than a million. Though the number of young people entering the labour market will slowly pick up again as we approach the year 2000, the deficit of young workers will continue until well into the next century.[5]

Under these circumstances, Britain has no choice but to make better use of the labour force she already has. A large and growing proportion of this labour force is female.

The growth of women's employment
Though women's labour inside and outside the home produces much of the wealth in all economies, in late twentieth century Britain women's contribution to the economy is particularly visible. Of the

new jobs that were created in the eighties the large majority were part-time jobs in service industries, and the bulk of them went to women. Women are taking less time out of work to raise their families, and more are returning to work in the intervals between the births of their children.[6]

The net result is that women are by far the most important source of growth in the country's workforce. In 1971, 36.5 per cent of all civilians in work in the UK were women; this rose to 40.6 per cent in 1981 and 43.1 per cent in 1988. By 1995, it is forecast that 44.4 per cent of all paid jobs will be done by women.

As every child knows, little girls grow up to be secretaries, nurses and shop assistants; boys grow up to be lorry drivers and deep-sea divers and many other different things as well. Compared to men, women are concentrated in a very narrow range of occupations, and most working women do jobs that are done only or nearly only by women.[7] Despite this, women have been increasing their representation in the world of work on a broad front. Table 1.1 classifies the workforce into nine major occupational groups, and shows that women's share of employment is increasing in seven of them. The only two occupational groups where women's share of employment is falling - craft and skilled manual occupations and plant and machine operatives - have both seen heavy job losses for men over the last two decades. Women now constitute over a quarter of managers and administrators, a third of professionals, well over two-fifths of associate professionals and technicians, going on for three-quarters of clerical and secretarial workers, around two-thirds of protective and personal service workers, more than three-fifths of sales workers, and approaching three-fifths of those in 'other occupations' (unskilled manual jobs, often cleaning, and agricultural work). By 1995, as the table shows, it is predicted that these proportions will be still higher.

In all the occupational groups that are expanding in the British economy, women's share of employment is also expanding. It is in employers' own interests to make the best use of this resource. Yet all the evidence tells the same tale, that women are being employed at levels well below their abilities.

Table 1.1 **Women as a percentage of all workers by occupation, 1971 to 1995**

	1971 %	1987 %	1995 %
Managers & administrators	20.7	26.4	28.1
Professional	31.9	33.5	34.0
Associate professional & technical	39.2	43.9	46.7
Clerical & secretarial	63.8	72.5	72.8
Craft and skilled manual	13.1	10.6	9.8
Protective & personal service	59.5	65.4	66.7
Sales	53.5	61.5	62.7
Plant & machine operatives	25.0	23.2	22.7
Other occupations	41.6	57.8	64.9
All in employment	36.5	43.1	44.4

Source: Institute for Employment Research 1989b, Table 5.

Note: Occupations classified by "Warwick Occupational Category".

Women's unused potential

The failure of women to reach their potential starts in school. Up to the age of 16, girls do better than boys academically. They get higher grades in examinations at 16 and are less likely to fail altogether; in the school year 1986-87 for example, 11 per cent of boys in England left school with no examination passes at all, compared to eight per cent of girls. Once past the minimum school leaving age, however, sex differences in achievement are reversed. Despite their poorer grades at age 16, more boys than girls succeed at the next hurdle: 16.9 per cent of boys leaving school in England in the school year 1986/87 had passed at least one A Level GCE, but only 16.3 per cent of girls had done so; 14.1 per cent of boy leavers had gained two or more A Levels, compared to 13.2 per cent of girls. From then on the gap between the sexes widens still further: 8.3 per cent of boys who left school in 1986/87 went on to a degree course; 6.6 per cent of girls did so. For boys this figure represented 57 per cent of all boys who left school with two or more A Levels; for girls it represented only 49 per cent.[8]

Even when women gain good academic qualifications, their chances of getting a job commensurate with their qualifications are smaller than the chances for men. Table 1.2 comes from a national government survey and compares the jobs of men and women with similar qualifications. The difference is striking. Forty-two per cent of economically active men (that is, men who are in work, or unemployed and seeking work) who have degree level qualifications

Table 1.2 Occupations of men and women with the same qualifications, GB 1987/88

Economically active persons aged 25-69 not in full-time education.

	Highest qualification obtained							
	degree or equivalent		higher education below degree level		GCE A Level or equivalent		GCE O Level or equivalent	
	men %	women %	men %	women %	men %	women %	men %	women %
Occupation								
Professional	42	15	15	1	7	1	2	0
Employers & managers	31	21	32	18	31	18	28	12
Intermediate non-manual	22	49	18	63	13	24	11	16
Junior non-manual	2	9	6	9	9	38	9	46
Skilled manual & own account non-professional	3	2	25	3	34	8	40	8
Semi-& unskilled manual & personal service	0	3	3	6	6	10	9	15
Total	100	100	100	100	100	100	100	100
Base N	1,330	569	1,258	917	1,182	450	1,593	1,685

Source: OPCS Social Survey Division (1990) Table 7.11b.

are employed in professional level jobs; the figure for economically active women graduates is 15 per cent. A further 31 per cent of economically active men with degrees are employers or managers, compared to just 21 per cent of women. The differential between the sexes is found all the way down the scale, even to the extent that 10 per cent of women with qualifications equivalent to GCE A Level and 15 per cent of women with O Levels or equivalent are working in semi-skilled and unskilled jobs. The wastage of talent that is implied by these figures is enormous.

Two conclusions are inescapable. First, there are a great many women who have the ability to do higher level jobs, but are barred from them by their lack of qualifications. Second, when women do get good qualifications, the jobs they get are often well below the jobs their education has fitted them for.

The problems of women returners

The reasons for women's under-achievement have been well explored by feminist writers. They have to do with gender socialisation and the curtailment of ambitions, with divisions in the labour market which class some jobs as women's work and others as work for men, with the identification of technology with masculinity, with indirect discrimination and the direct protection of male interests, and sometimes with unashamed prejudice. The influence of all these factors is profound, and is increased by the fact that it is still the norm that women take the main responsibility for caring for children and for sick and disabled relatives.

Most women who have a family take a break from paid work in order to care for their children; when they go back to work a large proportion move one or more rungs down the occupational ladder to less skilled and less responsible jobs. They are particularly likely to experience downward mobility if they have been away from work for a number of years, and if - as most do - they go back to work part-time. Part-time work fits in much better with the demands of family and home; unfortunately many part-time jobs in Britain are low skilled, badly paid, with poor conditions of employment and without the benefit of employment protection legislation. This problem was first brought to public view by the 'Women and Employment' study, a national survey of women's working lives carried out in 1980, which showed that 38 per cent of all women who did paid work at some time both before and after the birth of their first child returned to work after the birth at a level below that of the job they had held before.[9]

In the decade since the 'Women and Employment' study was carried out, there has been a growing trend for women to return to work more quickly after the birth of their first child. This trend has been encouraged by maternity rights legislation, which gives women who satisfy certain conditions the right to reinstatement in their old job, or the offer of a suitable alternative, once their maternity leave is over. Thus while in 1979 24 per cent of women who had worked during pregnancy were back at work within nine months of the birth of their baby, by 1988 the figure had risen to 45 per cent, 15 per cent of whom were working full-time and 29 per cent part-time.[10] Women who return to work quickly are much more likely than women who take an extended career break to return to a full-time job, and they have a far better chance of maintaining their position on the occupational ladder.

The trend is encouraging, but we are still a long way from seeing an end to the difficulties that face women when they are ready to resume paid employment. Although more women are returning to full-time work within a few months of the birth of a child, there has been no corresponding increase in the public provision of care for young children. Given the strains that the lack of good quality, secure and affordable childcare imposes, we do not know for how long these women will find themselves able to sustain their dual roles as workers and mothers. The Women and Employment study found that a third of mothers whose first return to work after the birth of their first child was full-time later switched to part-time work. Indeed, it is quite normal for employers who offer maternity pay above the statutory minimum to stipulate that the recipient must undertake to return to work for a specified period after the birth. Almost certainly some women return to work temporarily in order to retain this additional maternity pay, though they may be aware that they will be unable sustain the double burden of a job and a baby for very long. Even if a woman does succeed in this arduous endeavour, she almost certainly will have to reconsider her position if she has a second child.

Life is undoubtedly hard for most women who have a young family as well as a job. However even if a feminist fairy godmother could change the situation overnight and make it much easier for women to cope with this double role, there would still be many women who preferred to give up their job in order to look after their children full-time. In this respect as in others women have a right to choose. Thus public policy regarding women's employment should have twin goals: women who want or need to work while their children are small should be enabled to do so without undue hardship, and at the same time every effort should be made to ensure that the other talents of women who choose to make motherhood their full-time occupation for those few precious years while their children are small do not go permanently to waste.

For the foreseeable future the disruption in a woman's working life caused by the birth of children is likely to remain a major factor in the under-use of their abilities. Training for women returners can go a long way towards remedying the situation.

The need for adult training

Given the facts, it is vital for industry to make more effective use of women workers. It takes a long time to change society's perception of gender roles; in the meantime there are a number of very straightforward measures which could have an impact on how well women can use their abilities in paid work. A recent report commissioned by the Equal Opportunities Commission has put the case for flexible working arrangements, more open recruitment policies, care for children and other dependents, a restructuring of the financial incentives for work, and more investment in training.[11] Progress on any these fronts could set up a virtuous circle, allowing women to take on more responsible and more diverse roles at work, and steadily breaking down entrenched attitudes about what women are capable of. Unfortunately, while supportive statements abound, serious action is somewhat less common.

Training, then, is just one of a spectrum of measures that are called for, and this means training both at the point of transition between full-time education and work, and for adults who have already been in the labour market for some years. The need for training can arise at any one of a number of turning points in a woman's life, of which returning to work after a career break is just one. Training may also be called for when women are made redundant, when they are forced through the breakdown of a partnership or through widowhood to become the family's main breadwinner, when circumstances (such as moving home to follow the husband's employment) prevent them from continuing in their previous occupation, or to give them the chance to escape from low skill, low paid work. The Evaluation Study on which this book is founded demonstrates that carefully planned and properly funded adult training brings measurable gains for women. The gains would undoubtedly be greater if there were a co-ordinated policy effort to improve women's position in the labour force. Yet even in the absence of progress on other fronts, training can make an important contribution to the quality of women's working lives and to their earning power. This in turn increases both their incentive to work and their ability to pay for the facilities they require to balance the demands of home and job. At the same time adult training increases the economic value of women's work, and hence gives employers more incentive to provide the facilities and conditions of employment that will attract and keep women workers.

There is at the moment much public interest in training, and there have been calls to increase the country's investment in training from both government and opposition, and from both employers and trade unionists. The 1988 White Paper on 'Employment for the 1990's' stressed there was a need 'to set forward-looking training policies not just for young people but for everyone throughout their working lives'[12], while the Confederation of British Industry has affirmed that 'life-time learning is essential to enhance both business and people competitiveness'.[13] In effect, training today is the opposite of sin - everybody is for it. The questions on which there is less agreement are, who should take the lead, and who should pay the bill?

The pendulum of public policy

The position that the present Conservative administration has taken on adult skills training stands at one extreme of an arc through which the pendulum of government policy has swung more than once in the course of the century.[14] The latest swing has carried us back from the interventionist policies of the sixties and seventies to a revival of old style voluntarism.

Current government policy rests on the principle that the main beneficiaries of adult training are employers, and that therefore the provision of such training is first and foremost their responsibility. Training will, they maintain, be undertaken voluntarily by employers in their own best interests. Furthermore, the government believes that the market can provide the training that industry needs more efficiently and more effectively than a centrally planned and funded programme ever could. Thus the 1988 White Paper concluded that 'employers as both the providers and consumers of training have the primary responsibility for ensuring that our labour force has the skills to support our expanding economy'.[15] Employers can be encouraged by the state, but not interfered with. However the responsibility of the employer stops at the factory gate or office door, and that, according to the government, is where the responsibility of the individual takes over. According to the White Paper, individuals are to be encouraged 'to take responsibility for developing their own careers'.[16] The government acknowledges a role for the state only in providing a 'framework' for training, and in ensuring that some training is available for those individuals for whom employers will not provide, and who cannot provide for themselves, by whom it means primarily the long-term unemployed.

There have been times, however, when the state has taken a very different position with regard to adult training. During the two World Wars massive government training programmes were set up to meet the urgent needs of wartime production. Many thousands of women, who in peacetime were totally excluded from most craft apprenticeships, were trained in industrial skills both in special training units in factories and in government training centres. On both occasions emergency wartime measures failed to make any permanent impact on the traditional male dominated system of vocational education, and on the return of peace much of the state programme was closed down, whilst most of the surviving training centres devoted themselves to meeting the needs of soldiers returning to civilian life. The last war left behind a skeleton of skills training centres which continued to provide training in industrial skills for a smaller number of adults, most of whom were men.

In the sixties, the Labour government, worried by the inability of the traditional apprenticeship system to keep pace with an expanding economy and fast developing technology, reintroduced interventionist policies. The 1964 Industrial Training Act set up the Industry Training Boards, which were statutory bodies covering a wide range of industries, each with the power to raise a levy on the firms falling within its constituency. Funds collected in this way were returned to individual firms in the form of grants for specific training programmes approved by the Training Board. In this way the government attacked a perennial problem with vocational training, that some firms will leave others to spend money on training and then poach the workers as soon as they have been trained. The ITBs also spent considerable efforts on modernising the apprenticeship system by setting down standards for training and attaching conditions about the nature of the training provided to the grants that they distributed.

Though the work of the Industry Training Boards was very important, the need to upgrade the skills of the workforce was felt to be too urgent to wait until their achievements filtered through in succeeding generations of young people. Thus in the early seventies the government set up the Manpower Services Commission and gave it the job of greatly expanding the government's role as a direct provider of skills training for adults. One of the most important developments at this time was the launch of the Training Opportunities Programme - more commonly remembered as TOPS.

Though it built on the foundations of the Vocational Training Scheme which had survived from the Second World War, TOPS was in many ways a new departure. Courses were open to all men or women aged 19 or more who had been out of full-time education for at least three years, and who were either not in work or were willing to give up their job in order to take training. The courses enabled adults who had been out of work for some time to refresh, update or upgrade their skills and so re-enter employment; they also provided an opportunity for people who wished to change the kind of work they did, or who wanted to advance in their chosen occupation. The courses gave intensive off-the-job training in a very wide range of subjects, at all levels from the semi-skilled to the professional. They lasted anything from a month to a year, and were held in government skills centres, in colleges, and in private training institutions. A training allowance, not generous but enough to live on, was payable as of right to all full-time trainees and was not means-tested. As the programme developed, special 'returners' courses were introduced for women who had not worked for several years. Many of these courses were part-time, and offered help which was particularly appropriate to the situation in which these women found themselves, such as attention to building their confidence in themselves and help with job search and interview techniques.

TOPS was a popular programme, and there was some competition to get onto the courses. By the second half of the 1970's around 90,000 adults were completing training every year. Forty-three per cent of these were women.

With the rise to power of Mrs Thatcher's government in 1979 the pendulum swung back from interventionism to voluntarism. The new administration disliked what it saw as the 'compulsion and bureaucracy' of the Industrial Training Boards, and in 1981 all but seven of the 23 Boards were wound up.[17] In their place a network of voluntary organisations was given the task of co-ordinating training arrangements within industrial sectors. Six of the surviving Training Boards are now soon to be abolished; only in the construction industry will statutory powers be retained. Not surprisingly, the Thatcher government also questioned the value of TOPS.

By the early 1980's unemployment was climbing to record levels, and public attention turned from planning for future skills needs to coping with the crisis represented by three million out of work. Just as in the Great Depression of the inter-war years, training began once more to be used as a way of softening the impact of mass unemployment. Young people were particularly hard hit by the recession, and initially most of the government's efforts were directed into the Youth Opportunities Programme and its successor, the Youth Training Scheme. Meanwhile the number of adults who were long term unemployed grew steadily, and as the decade progressed programmes were launched specifically for them. The Community Programme gave part-time work at union rates, sometimes accompanied by training, though more often not so. This was displaced in 1985 by the short-lived New Job Training Scheme aimed at the under-25's, and in 1988 a number of separate initiatives for adults were brought together under the comprehensive Employment Training programme. Eligibility for all these programmes was based on long-term registered unemployment, and on all of them the majority of participants were men.

In order to fund the new programmes, resources were gradually withdrawn from TOPS and the number of trainees began to fall. In 1985 the programme was repackaged and relaunched as the Job Training Scheme, with a greater emphasis on market responsiveness, but it was almost immediately renamed the Old Job Training Scheme, or OJTS, to distinguish it from the New Job Training Scheme which was set up shortly afterwards. The New Job Training Scheme was a very different kind of programme from TOPS: it was aimed primarily at under-25's who were long-term unemployed, it was intended to operate mainly through work placements with employers, and trainees received only the means-tested social security benefits they were entitled to plus a nominal training allowance. The scheme ran into a lot of opposition from the trade union movement, which feared that employers would use it to force down wage rates and substitute trainees for permanent employees. The New Job Training Scheme had only a brief lifespan, but a number of the ideas which inspired it lived on in the new and much larger programme which took its place, the Employment Training programme or ET.

TOPS lingered for a year or two more under its new name of OJTS. However OJTS was expensive in comparison to the new schemes - in 1986 the average cost per person completing training under OJTS was £4,216, of which sum training allowances constituted 32.8 per cent and course fees 67.2 per cent.[18] Moreover, despite its repackaging, the government still believed that the programme was inefficient. Eventually OJTS was swallowed altogether by ET, to the regret of many who trained under it or helped in its running. Within ET there survives a small corner of high technology training which perpetuates some of the principles of TOPS, though on a much reduced scale, with just 7,000 trainees in the financial year 1989/90.[19] Now that control of ET has been devolved to the network of local employer-led Training and Enterprise Councils (known in Scotland as Local Enterprise Companies), the future of even this small corner is uncertain, particularly in view of the substantial budget cuts that the TECs have had to cope with since they were first created.

No place for a woman?

The shift from TOPS/OJTS to ET has closed off an important route which many women used to get a better foothold in the world of work. It has resulted in a squeeze on places for women in adult training.

This situation has arisen because the main eligibility criterion for entry to ET has been long-term unemployment. Mainstream entrants to ET, to whom the large majority of places are allocated, have been divided into the 'guarantee' group - people aged 18 to 24 who have been registered unemployed for six months - and the 'aim group', consisting of people aged 25 to 59 who have been registered unemployed for two years or more, who come next in priority. However fewer unemployed women than unemployed men register at

Job Centres or Employment Offices, because they are less likely to be eligible for unemployment benefit. Women tend to have more interruptions in their working lives than men and can find it more difficult to build up the record of National Insurance contributions on which eligibility for unemployment benefit is based, and many women also have earnings which are so low that they fall outside the National Insurance system altogether. As a result many unemployed women do not qualify for a mainstream place on ET.

Women returners were another important group who were well catered for by TOPS/OJTS. During the first few years of ET, a small proportion of the funding was set aside for non-mainstream groups, for whom the normal eligibility requirement of long-term registered unemployment was waived. Returners (defined as people who had been away from work for more than two years) were included here, along with people with disabilities, people whose first language was not English, and members of HM Forces returning to civilian life. The number of women returners receiving training on ET was much smaller than under TOPS/OJTS, and since its launch ET has been subjected to a series of budget cuts. Places for returners, regarded as both expensive and marginal to the main functions of ET, have been amongst those most vulnerable. Very recently, the distinction between mainstream and non-mainstream places on ET has been dropped, and no-one yet knows how this will affect the relative provision for men and women.

The particular needs of women returners mean that the demand for training is very great amongst women in their thirties and forties. Thus the fact that the eligibility criteria for ET favour the under-25's also disadvantages women. On TOPS/OJTS, 32 per cent of male trainees were under 25, but only 23 per cent of female trainees were as young as this.

The impact of the eligibility criteria for ET can be seen in the figures. In the mid-1980s around 45 per cent of trainees on TOPS/OJTS were women; today the proportion of women trainees on ET is 31 per cent.[20] The loss of places for women reflects the fact that the proportion of men on TOPS/OJTS who satisfied the eligibility criteria for ET (18 per cent) was half as big again as the corresponding proportion of women (12 per cent).[21]

Since the 1988 White Paper the government's direct role in training has been progressively reduced, and most of the powers and the funds have been devolved to the local Training and Enterprise Councils. These are a network of around 80 independent companies funded by the government and charged with promoting training activities by industry and delivering government funded training schemes. Each TEC is run by a board of directors drawn primarily from amongst chief executives and managing directors of large local companies. In his autumn budget statement of 1990 the Chancellor of the Exchequer announced another reduction in the government budget for training - a cut of £365 million from a budget of £1.2 billion. Many TEC directors were already unhappy with the way the budget they had originally been promised had been whittled away, and so to sweeten the pill the TECs were given even more flexibility than they had before in the ways in which they could spend government money. The extent of the powers now devolved to the TECs makes it difficult to foresee how government funds for training will be deployed in the future.

Whatever statements the government might make about the importance of training for women, there is no reason to suppose that their needs will be rated at all highly as the TECs draw up their plans. Because of the way that the TEC boards of directors are constituted, there are very few women indeed amongst them. At the time of writing, throughout the whole country only one TEC board is chaired by a woman.

Other provision for women

According to the government, the responsibility for providing adult training belongs first and foremost to employers, next to individuals, and only residually to the government itself. If employers were able and willing to assume this responsibility with regards to women, and if individual women had the resources to finance their own training, then the loss of places for women on government training programmes would not matter. If, on the other hand, training for women is being neglected, then the government needs to reconsider its position on whether it should invest directly in adult training for a wider range of people than just the long-term unemployed.

In general, the record of British employers as providers of training is not good. A recent report has shown that even in the fastest growing sector of the economy, banking and finance, expenditure on training per employee (excluding the employee's wages) increased by only 0.4

per cent between 1984 and 1988, and this followed a drop in spending in 1981 to 1984. In construction and manufacturing industry, spending on training did not grow at all. In relation to total labour costs, spending in the UK on vocational training in manufacturing fell from 1.8 per cent in 1981 to 1.3 per cent in 1988 - a period during which our major European competitors maintained or increased their expenditure.[22]

If employers do not spend enough on training generally, it is women who get the worst deal. A recent analysis of national data has established that young women suffer considerable discrimination in access to training. After taking account of their age, qualifications, region, the size of the establishment, the industry in which they were employed, and the length of time they had been in the job, this analysis showed that young women's chances of receiving training were reduced by a third or more in comparison with young men, and their chances of receiving training specific to the job they were in were reduced by one half or more. The same analysis also showed that, other things being equal, women employees who were married or who had young children were significantly less likely to receive training than either other women employees or men.[23]

The Equal Opportunities Commission, worried by the direction which government policy has taken, has recently completed a wide-ranging review of training provision for women.[24] The review concluded that although the proportion of women receiving job-related training has increased over the last decade, the unmet demand for training is substantial amongst older women and amongst women who are poorly qualified. It found that most of the training provided by employers is offered to young women and to women who already have good qualifications. In addition, women in part-time jobs were shown to have only half the chances that women working full-time have of getting training. The review also reported a very high level of demand for training amongst women with family commitments who want to return to paid work, the demand being particularly great for part-time courses. There also appeared to be a dearth of information and guidance about any opportunities that might already exist.

If employers are not providing enough training, can the shortfall be made up by individual women paying for their own training? This is precisely what the government hopes will happen, and as encouragement, in 1988 it set up a scheme for 'Career Development Loans'. Under this scheme applicants can obtain a loan of up to £5,000 from a commercial bank to cover 80 per cent of the cost of course fees and certain other expenses for up to a year of study on a vocational training course. The student is given a 'repayment holiday' while on the course and for up to three months afterwards, during which time the interest on the loan is paid by the Employment Department. After that time both the capital and any further interest must be repaid within a period negotiated with the bank concerned.

Career Development Loans could be attractive to people who want to t···in for a well-paid job and who are confident both of their ability to succeed on the training course and their chances of finding employment afterwards; it is however unlikely to be a realistic proposition for the many women who feel that training would help them to return to work after a career break. Most women in this position have already been through a period when the family income has been reduced by the loss of the wife's earnings, and it is often the growing demands on that reduced income that make them think of going back to work. The last thing they are likely to want to do is to increase the financial pressures on the family by going into debt. Moreover, many women returners have lost confidence in themselves, and would not regard their future career prospects as bright enough to enable them to pay off a loan without difficulty. And however bright the prospects, most mothers on the brink of returning to work after some years can only view the step as an experiment, whose success depends on factors over which they have little control - how well child care arrangements work out, how the family reacts to the change, how often their children are off school. It is rare for a woman returner confidently to expect that the step will prove successful and permanent - yet the expectation must be very secure to justify the family going into debt to finance her training. What is more, women who take out a loan need future earnings which are high enough to enable them to repay it, while still making a contribution to the family income that justifies the extra strains imposed by going out to work - but women's hourly earnings are around two-thirds of male earnings.

The unviability of the scheme for most women is proved by the take-up figures. In the two years and four months the scheme had been running up to December 1990, only 13,000 loans were made, and only 30 per cent of these went to women.[25] This works out at an average of around 1,700 women getting loans each year - indeed a drop in the ocean. According to one of the banks involved in the scheme, the most popular jobs for re-trainees are computer programmers, hairdressers, airline pilots and driving instructors.[26] It is not hard to guess which trainees are women.

The government thinks it right that employers should supply the training that women need, and that, where employers fail, women should pay for that training themselves. Unfortunately for women, this view seems to rest more on hope than on reality.

Building on past experience

The TOPS/OJTS programme was very helpful to many women who felt they needed adult training. One commentator, writing in the late seventies when TOPS was still in full swing, characterised it in the following terms:

> The MSC-financed TOPS scheme is the programme most suited to the training needs of women re-entrants and most widely used by them...This programme was specifically developed to meet the needs of those wishing to acquire a new skill, update a rusty one, or train for a new occupation.[27]

Nevertheless the scheme was not without its problems. Apart from the cost to the public purse, the main difficulties concerned the transition from training to employment. Men who had been trained in the traditional crafts sometimes met opposition from apprentice-trained men who felt that TOPS/OJTS gave a short cut to skilled status. Lack of experience in a real workplace could also present problems when it came to applying on-the-job the skills that had been learned only in the classroom. The Manpower Services Commission's own internal review of TOPS towards the end of the seventies proposed better publicity of the range of courses available, more part-time provision, more short term preparation-for-work courses to improve employability, and more attention to assistance in finding a job and bridging the job/training gap. These proposals had only started to be put into effect when the whole TOPS/OJTS programme was overtaken by budget cuts and eventually closed down.

Times change, and the solutions to the problems of the seventies and the eighties are not necessarily applicable in the nineties. At the same time, viable programmes cannot be invented overnight, but must build on what has gone before. Where the training needs of women were concerned, TOPS/OJTS had a good deal of experience to offer, and lessons can be learned from the programme that are still valid today.

However, the government's stance on adult training is more radical than a simple rejection of a particular mode of delivery: it has declared its unwillingness to fund training for any but the long-term unemployed. This stance is based partly on a generalised faith in market principles, partly on the competition for funds from unemployment based programmes, and partly on the conviction that centrally planned and funded training is bound to be wasteful and unresponsive to the needs of industry. Yet when TOPS/OJTS was abandoned, there was no conclusive evidence either to support or refute this charge.

The MSC had for many years conducted regular follow-up studies of the destinations of TOPS/OJTS trainees three months after leaving training. In the financial year 1985/1986 these surveys showed that 57 per cent of trainees found work in jobs which used the skills in which they had trained.[28] However no-one knew what happened to these men and women after three months, nor how many would have found work anyway, regardless of whether they had taken part in the programme or not. In 1986 the MSC decided to commission an evaluation of TOPS/OJTS which attempted to answer both of these questions.

The Evaluation Study
Though TOPS/OJTS was being run down at the time the new study was commissioned, in 1986 it was still fully operational and almost 40,000 trainees completed training under the programme. The Evaluation Study was based on 785 trainees - 377 women and 408 men - who were selected in such a way as to form a representative sample of all trainees in Great Britain who completed courses in the last two quarters of 1986. These men and women were interviewed during September and October 1987, and were contacted a second time by post in the spring of 1988. On the basis of information collected in the interview, the trainees were matched with a comparison sample consisting of people who had experienced similar patterns of employment up until 1986, but who had not had any training in recent years. This comparison sample was located by means of a screening procedure based on interviews with a large and

21

nationally representative sample of individuals. The study also analysed administrative data for a nationally representative sample of 2,710 trainees. Details of how the study was carried out are given in Appendix One.

The findings of the Evaluation Study were published by the Training Agency in 1990.[29] The implications of the study for government training policy remained to be spelled out. This book is about the relevance of the findings to the training needs of women, and the conclusions that follow for public investment in women's skills.

Notes to Chapter One
1. The forecasts quoted in this paragraph and elsewhere in the chapter are by a team of economists at Warwick University (Institute for Employment Research 1989a and 1989b)
2. Smith, E. (1990).
3. Department of Education and Science (1990).
4. National Institute of Economic and Social Research (1989).
5. Employment Department (1988).
6. Martin, J. and Roberts, C. (1984); McRae, S. (1991).
7. Hakim, C. (1979); Martin, J. and Roberts, C. (1984).
8. Department of Education and Science (1988).
9. Martin, J. and Roberts, C. (1984).
10. McRae, S. (1991).
11. Metcalf, H. and Leighton, P. (1989).
12. Employment Department (1988), p3.
13. Confederation of British Industry (1989), p18.
14. The historical material in this chapter is drawn from Sheldrake, J. and Vickerstaff, S. (1987), who give a fascinating and scholarly account of the twentieth century history of public training policy in Britain.
15. Employment Department (1988), p59.
16. Employment Department (1988), p52.
17. O'Connell, B. (1990).
18. Manpower Services Commission internal report on the 1986 Cost Efficiency and Cost Effectiveness Exercise.
19. Wilson, J. (1990).
20. Employment Department (1990a).

21. Calculations from the Evaluation Study described later in the chapter.
22. McLeish, H. (1990).
23. Green, F., (1991).
24. Clarke, K., (1991).
25. Figures supplied by the Employment Department.
26. The Observer, Feb. 17 1991, p32.
27. Rothwell, S. (1980), p197.
28. Manpower Services Commission internal report: 'The Job Training Scheme Follow-up Surveys: Results for courses completed during the financial year 1985/86', September 1986.
29. Payne, J. (1990).

2. Women's Need for Training

Although the main aim of the Evaluation Study was to assess the impact that taking part in the successor to TOPS, the Old Job Training Scheme, had on trainees' lives, this could not be achieved without first trying to understand what led them to seek training. This exploration is also the starting point from which the case for public investment in adult training for women is developed, for it shows that their need for training often arose out of their experiences as women, and as mothers and wives.

This chapter will describe a number of themes which were commonly found in women's decisions to seek training. However, in addition to these commonly recurring elements, there was also a wide diversity of motives and of circumstances, and we must begin with the question of why it was that TOPS/OJTS was so popular with women and why it attracted women from so many different walks of life. The answer lies in the philosophy behind TOPS/OJTS and the way that this shaped the programme.

Two different philosophies
As the last chapter showed, the philosophy behind TOPS/OJTS differed fundamentally from the conviction of the superiority of market processes which has determined recent government policy towards adult training. It is the old debate between interventionism and voluntarism which has characterised so many political developments during the Thatcher years. TOPS/OJTS was founded on the belief that society as a whole reaps the benefits of a skilled workforce, and that therefore society as a whole should share the costs of creating those skills. The market philosophy asserts that the main beneficiaries of training are individual employers and individual workers; hence they should pay the largest share of the bill. TOPS/OJTS was based on the belief that to ensure that the economy has the skills it needs for growth there must be long-term planning for

training needs, and it was maintained that this could be achieved only by government intervention. Left to themselves, employers could be expected to provide only for their most immediate and short-term requirements. The market philosophy argues that individual employers know best what their training needs are, and in pursuit of their own long-term interests will provide the training that they need. It further holds that central planning is inevitably bureaucratic and leads to inappropriate provision.

These differences in philosophy are very apparent in the contrast between TOPS/OJTS and Employment Training, or ET, which is currently by far the most important government initiative in the field of adult training. Whereas TOPS/OJTS was run first and foremost as a training programme and was seen as such, a persistent public perception of ET, despite advertising campaigns, is that it is primarily a way of keeping the unemployed off the unemployment register. TOPS/OJTS gave full-time training off-the-job in classrooms and training workshops, with little if any involvement by employers; the training it offered was sometimes charged with being out of touch with market needs, but it was never accused of not being real training. ET tries to ensure relevance to market needs by aiming to provide all trainees with work placements, though in fact placements with employers have proved difficult to secure in adequate numbers, and only a minority of trainees are given them - more get their practical work on special projects.[1] Where employer placements are available, critics allege that employers can use trainees as cheap labour, displacing waged workers and providing little or no real training. This allegation has been lent force by the fact that although, when ET was first launched, all ET trainees were guaranteed a minimum of 40 per cent of 'directed' training, either on-the-job or off-the-job, this guarantee was later dropped. There is in fact no obligation for employers who take on ET trainees to provide them with any off-the-job training at all.

Other differences between the two programmes also reflect their different ideologies. TOPS/OJTS was designed to open up training to as many people as possible, and so all full-time trainees were paid a training allowance to cover subsistence; the allowance was not means-tested and was set at a level comfortably above the rates for unemployment benefit.[2] ET trainees in contrast receive only the means-tested social security benefits they are eligible for, plus a training allowance of £10. If they are not eligible for benefits, £10 is all they receive. Taking part in TOPS/OJTS was wholly voluntary, and indeed there was some competition to get onto the programme; participation in ET is usually suggested to trainees by their local Employment Office after they have been unemployed for a certain length of time, and is backed by the sanction that in some circumstances refusal to take up a place can lead to loss of benefit. TOPS/OJTS was open to everybody, including people who were already in work, as long as they were willing to give up their job to go on the course. On ET, only the long-term unemployed have ever been guaranteed a place, and though a small proportion of places has been set aside for other 'non-mainstream' groups, the scheme has never been open to people who are already employed.

The TOPS/OJTS philosophy meant that there were few formal restrictions on entry: the main criteria for selection were a desire to train, an ability to benefit from training, and an undertaking to seek to use the training received in subsequent employment. Nor did the scheme carry any stigma of compulsion or association with unemployment - unemployed men and women went onto to TOPS/OJTS because they believed they would gain from it, and they trained side-by-side with men and women who were sufficiently well motivated towards training to give up a job in order to do their course. As a result the scheme attracted a very wide range of entrants, both men and women.

These, then, were the principles that guided training provision on TOPS/OJTS in 1986 when the sample of trainees for the Evaluation study was drawn. We turn now to a description of the women amongst them. These women were scattered geographically across the length and breadth of Britain, but there are many common threads in the ways in which their need for training arose out of their past histories and current circumstances.

The backgrounds of women trainees

The ages of women trainees on TOPS/OJTS in 1986 ranged from 19 to 59, though two thirds were between 25 and 44. They tended to be older than men trainees on the programme - their average age was 34 and 46 per cent were over 35, whereas the men had an average age of 31, and only 28 per cent were over 35. In many cases they had been prevented from taking training sooner by the age of their children. Just under two-thirds of women on TOPS/OJTS were married, a fifth were single, and 14 per cent were separated, divorced or widowed. Two thirds had children; their families ranged in age from toddlers to grown ups with children of their own. Most commonly the youngest child was at primary school or had just started secondary education. Their family commitments were very closely bound up with their working lives, and figured largely in the explanation of why they sought adult training now.

The majority of women trainees were not in work before they started their course. Thirty-seven per cent said they were unemployed in the month before their course started, and 25 per cent said they had been 'doing something else', most usually looking after family and home. These are the women who in official statistics would be classed as 'economically inactive'. However the distinction between being unemployed and being economically inactive is not always very clear for women. Many women who would like to work but cannot find a job do not have sufficient National Insurance contributions to entitle them to unemployment benefit, and so do not register as unemployed. Thus it is best to look first of all simply at how long it was since these women had last worked, regardless of the words they chose to describe their situation.

In this respect there was a marked contrast between male and female trainees, for it had generally been much longer since the women had last held a job. Seventy per cent of male trainees were not in employment in the month before they started training, but 45 per cent had worked within the year and only 25 per cent had been away from work for longer. Sixty-four per cent of women trainees were not working in the month before their course, but only 26 per cent had been in employment during the previous twelve months and 38 per cent had been away from work for more than a year. Indeed, 13 per cent of women had been out of work for more than five years compared to only two per cent of male trainees. Sometimes the gap in women's employment had been very long indeed: absences of eleven or twelve years were not uncommon, and there were two women in the Evaluation Study who had not worked for over twenty years. In addition, some eight per cent of women trainees had never done any paid work at all, compared to only two per cent of men. These included a number of young women without families who had left school at a time of very high unemployment, as well as some older women who had not worked before their first child was born.

Women returners

Women returners thus formed a very important client group for TOPS/OJTS. Seven-eighths of women who had not been in work before their course had families, and 17 per cent of women with children had not worked during the five years before the start of their course, compared to only five per cent of women trainees who had no children. Women whose youngest child had not yet started secondary school tended to have had the longest gaps in employment - more than a fifth of women trainees with children this age had not worked during the five years before their course.

Mrs C., from a remote area in Wales, was one of the women for whom training provided a route back into work after being a full-time housewife for a great many years. In her case, as in all the case studies presented in this book, some personal details have been changed to make sure that she cannot be identified, but the essential points about her experience have been retained. She was qualified as a radiographer but had given up her job when she was pregnant with her first child; she had a second son four years later and had not worked for 17 years. With her children grown up she wanted to go out to work again, but found that she could not get back into radiography: 'So I decided to get some secretarial skills to see where that led'. She learned about TOPS/OJTS from a neighbour, and did a six month part-time college course in business studies and office arts. This gained her qualifications in elementary bookkeeping, typing and word processing. Despite these, and despite being given a lot of help by her college tutors in how to look for work , it took her several months to get a job. In the end, however, she secured a post as a part-time clerical officer with her local health authority. She wrote the following about her course:

> Apart from learning new skills and obtaining additional qualifications, the course helped me to regain the confidence which I had before leaving full-time employment, 17 years earlier, in order to bring up a family.

Mrs M., a Yorkshirewoman, had worked as a secretary before she had her family, but like many women had been obliged to settle for less skilled and less well paid part-time work while her two children were small. She had taken a job as a playgroup supervisor, which she had to leave when she injured her back, and later worked as a school meals supervisor in a small primary school. She 'got fed up' with this second position, and had been without a job for two years when she started her course. However she wanted to work again and followed up a newspaper advertisement for TOPS/OJTS 'because I didn't think I would get an office job without re-training'. She did a part-time shorthand/typing refresher course, gaining qualifications in shorthand and word processing, and found work very quickly afterwards. Her new employer was a firm of civil engineers, and she described herself as 'very satisfied' with her job: 'I run the office completely'. When we last heard from her in spring 1989 she had been in this job over two years. She wrote that training:

> ...gives back confidence, and I'm sure employers are more inclined to give an interview to someone who has taken the course as a first step in returning to work after a long absence.

Unemployment

Though the distinction between unemployment and economic inactivity is often unclear for women, nevertheless there were differences between the women who described themselves as unemployed before they started their course and the women who had also not been in paid work but said they were 'doing something else', by which they usually meant looking after home and family. The former tended to be younger - nearly a third were under 25 compared to a mere six per cent of full-time housewives - and they were also less likely to be married (61 per cent as against 85 per cent of housewives). However the biggest difference between the two groups was that more than half of the women who described themselves as unemployed had no children, or no children who were still living at home, whereas virtually all the full-time housewives had children at home.

Roughly one in ten of both unemployed women and housewives had never had a job, but this apart, the unemployed women had generally been away from work for a much shorter time. Fifty-four per cent of unemployed women had worked within the previous twelve months, compared to 22 per cent of housewives, and only seven per cent of unemployed women had been away from work for more than five years, compared to 44 per cent of housewives.

One unemployed woman who found TOPS/OJTS training helpful was Miss McN. from Edinburgh. She was 28 and unmarried, and lived with her brother's family. Her educational qualifications were not good, and she had never had a proper job. After many years out of work she was sent by the Job Centre on a week-long Restart course, and it was the instructor there who suggested she apply for a place on TOPS/OJTS. She said she had wanted to get training a long time ago, but was 'unaware that I could apply for a course - at that time there was less publicity about these things'. She completed a short elementary word processing course, gaining a Pitman's certificate. The value of this course for her was that it 'gave me the confidence to apply for jobs and attend interviews, whereas beforehand I had no confidence at all'. At the end of the course she went back on the dole, but at the same time started to work as an unpaid volunteer in a housing co-operative. Her story has a moderately happy ending, for after four months of voluntary work she was offered a full-time paid position as a clerical assistant. Though at first she was 'a little dissatisfied' with this job, she stayed with it and began to get to like it more.

Mrs W., a young woman from the South East, was also unemployed before her course but was led into adult training by a rather different set of circumstances. She had A Levels and good secretarial qualifications and had worked for several years as a secretary in a large company. However she became increasingly dissatisfied with her career, which she felt did not use her abilities properly. The 'last straw' was a repetitive strain injury to her hands, which she attributed to the ever-increasing amount of typing she had to do, and which ultimately forced her to give up her job. After a period of unemployment she applied for a course in COBOL programming. Though the three-month course did not lead to any formal qualification, she had to wait only a month at the end of it before securing a full-time job as a computer programmer with an insurance company. She liked this job very much, and was sent by the company on a series of week long courses to improve her skills in COBOL. She wrote:

> The course enabled me to enter into a career for which I am suited. It proved my ability, so that my company ... felt it worthwhile investing further monies in work related training.

Working women
In the Evaluation Study, just over a third of women trainees came to their course straight from a job. They were a little less likely to be married or to have children than other women on TOPS/OJTS, and those who did have children tended to have older children; these differences however were not very great. These women sought training not because they wanted to return to work after a long interruption or to escape from unemployment: their motivation was rather that they were dissatisfied with their jobs and felt that they could do better if they acquired new skills, and in particular, if they got to grips with the new technology in office work.

This dissatisfaction was evident in their work histories, for many had changed jobs several times in the years leading up to their course. Three fifths had worked for more than one employer since 1980, including two fifths who had worked for three or more employers and a quarter for four or more. Very often the jobs they left in order to enter training were low skilled and poorly paid. Nearly half of them worked as sales assistants or check-out cashiers, or in low skilled jobs in catering, cleaning and other personal service occupations, and another eight per cent did factory work; only a third were employed in clerical or secretarial jobs. Their jobs contrasted sharply with the last occupations of women who were full-time housewives before starting their course, two thirds of whom had previously been in clerical or secretarial work. Indeed, women who went into training straight from a job tended to be working at a lower skill level even than that of the last jobs of women who were unemployed before their course.

In many cases women who entered TOPS/OJTS straight from a job had done more skilled work before their children were born. These women could not be classed as 'returners' according to the definition that is used for entry to ET because they had already gone back to work again, and a 'returner' on ET is someone who has been away from work for more than two years. Nevertheless their training needs were very similar to those of women returners. Mrs L., for example, aged 40 and a mother of three, had been a secretary before she had a family, but worked for many years as a home help while her children were young. When she developed back trouble, she looked to TOPS/OJTS for an opportunity to 'brush up' her skills and so return to secretarial work. Enabling women like Mrs L. to go back to skilled work was a very important function of the training programme.

Sometimes, however, it was changed circumstances that prompted the step into training. Mrs V. had been employed as a machinist in the fashion trade all her life, but on moving out of London with her husband found that job opportunities were restricted. She managed to get another job, but said, 'I disliked it very much - I was exploited'. In the area she had moved to there were much better jobs to be had in the electronics industry, and she enrolled on a course in basic electronics in order to switch to this line of work.

In other cases, women simply wanted to get on in the world. This was the motivation for Mrs M., a secretary who was ambitious to go further in her career, but who found her path blocked because she did not have shorthand: 'I couldn't get the jobs I wanted without it'. Other women needed training to widen an otherwise restricted range of options. Since her children came along, Mrs A's world had been particularly narrow. She had worked from home for some years making and selling dolls, but now wanted to get out into the world outside. She took a course in updating business skills, after which she was able to obtain a job as production manager in an advertising firm.

Lone mothers

A seventh of the women trainees on TOPS/OJTS were lone parents. Compared to other women trainees with children, lone mothers were young - one in five was under 25 compared to only one in fifty of mothers with partners. Their families were also smaller: half of lone mothers had only one child compared to a quarter of mothers with partners. The lone mothers were more likely to be in work in the month before they started their training course (44 per cent as against 30 per cent of mothers with partners), and if they were not in work, they were less likely to have been out of work for a very long time - only eight per cent had been away from work for more than five years compared to 20 per cent of mothers with partners. A half of lone mothers were working or had last worked in low skill occupations in selling and personal service, compared to a little over a quarter of mothers with partners.

Ms J. and Ms K. were not untypical of the younger lone mothers who trained on TOPS/OJTS. Ms J. had been forced to leave school prematurely when she became pregnant, though she had returned to sit her examinations and had two CSEs. Since then she had been fully occupied caring for her daughter, and had never had a paid job. When the child was three she did a short course in sewing machining, and she planned to look for work when her child started school. Ms K. was 17 when she became pregnant and was working as a waitress, despite her four O Levels. She returned to work when the baby was two, and had held a number of part-time jobs, usually in the hotel and catering trade. She decided to train because 'I wanted to get a skill so I could earn decent money in a full-time job'. The new town where she lived offered opportunities for women in the electronics industry, and a six week course in printed circuit board assembly secured her the kind of work she had aimed for.

To lone mothers who were still young TOPS/OJTS offered the chance to gain a skill for the first time; to those who were older, and usually separated or divorced, it offered the opportunity to refresh or update a skill they already possessed. The situation of these women was often similar to that of married women who wanted to return to the type of work they had done before their children were born, except that their need to earn good money was more urgent. Mrs D., for example, had started her career as a medical secretary. She was divorced not long after her second child was born, and following this had worked for many years as a school kitchen assistant as this was the only work she could combine with her domestic situation. When the children were old enough to be left alone she took a refresher course in shorthand typing 'to get a career for myself again', and after a series of short-term jobs she eventually attained the kind of work she was looking for. She wrote:

> I am now employed in the capacity I was in before I had my children
> ... I would never have had the capacity or confidence to do this without
> this course.

Mrs T's circumstances were similar: she had two teenage children, was divorced, and had worked part-time as a home help for several years despite good secretarial qualifications. She took a secretarial refresher course 'because I didn't want to be a home help for the rest of my life', but though she intended eventually to return to work, at the time of the interview she had not yet started looking for a job.

33

Educational background

As will be evident by now, women who trained on TOPS/OJTS came from a wide variety of educational backgrounds. To some extent this reflected the diversity of the courses that were included in the scheme, but it was also a result of deliberate selection policies for applicants. Though previous experience was always helpful in gaining a place on a course, applicants were not excluded from applying simply because they lacked formal educational qualifications. For applicants to computing courses there was a standard aptitude test that was used for courses throughout the country, and one of the explicit reasons why this test was used was to 'help break down "artificial" academic barriers to training'.[3] For clerical and secretarial courses there were tests of English and arithmetic that could be used when applicants did not have appropriate educational qualifications. These selection procedures gave a second chance to men and women who had failed in school.

Though three-fifths of women trainees on TOPS/OJTS had left school at 16 or younger, many women trainees had stayed in education beyond the minimum leaving age, and one in ten had been in full-time education up to the age of 20 or beyond. The educational qualifications of trainees were correspondingly diverse: there were women with degrees, with teaching diplomas or nursing qualifications, and advanced vocational qualifications such as university diplomas, membership of professional associations and Higher National Certificates or Diplomas. Though some women had qualifications like these in scientific or technical subjects, most were in fields more traditionally occupied by women, such as the paramedical professions, domestic science or music. In addition, a number of women trainees had qualifications in shorthand, typing and other clerical or secretarial skills. In total, a fifth of women trainees on TOPS/OJTS had qualifications at GCE A Level standard or higher, a little under two fifths had qualifications equivalent to GCE O Level, a fifth had other qualifications either below O Level standard or gained abroad and not classifiable with British qualifications, and just over a fifth had no formal educational qualifications at all. Younger trainees were more likely to have qualifications than their older colleagues, and in this respect they mirrored the population nationally, for there has been a large rise in the number of young people gaining qualifications since the school leaving age was raised from 15 to 16 in 1973.

Although the range of qualifications held by women trainees was wide, it was not as wide as in the economically active workforce as a

Table 2.1 Qualifications of women trainees on TOPS/OJTS compared with the qualifications of all women in GB who were in work or unemployed in 1986, by age

	highest qualification held					
	above A level standard %	A level standard %	below A level standard %	no qualifi- cations %	%	Total (N)
Age 20-29:						
Women trainees	8	14	62	16	100	(129)
All women in GB in work or unemployed	18	15	54	13	100	(1,301)
Age 30-39:						
Women trainees	7	12	55	26	100	(116)
All women in GB in work or unemployed	22	6	37	35	100	(1,280)
Age 40-49:						
Women trainees	5	14	54	26	100	(90)
All women in GB in work or unemployed	16	3	35	46	100	(1,078)
All aged 20-49:						
Women trainees	7	13	57	22	100	(335)
All unemployed women in GB	16	7	39	38	100	(287)

Sources: GB figures: OPCS Social Survey Division (1989) Table 9.17 (own calculations).
Women trainees: Evaluation Study.

whole. Table 2.1 compares trainees with all women who were either working, or unemployed seeking work, in Great Britain in 1986. In each of the three age groups in which there were enough women trainees to permit the comparison, there were fewer women trainees with qualifications above A Level standard than was the case for economically active women as a whole. In addition, in the two older age groups there were fewer trainees with no qualifications at all, though this was not true for trainees aged 20 to 29. The last two rows of the table compare women trainees aged 20 to 49 to unemployed women only, and shows that relative to them also, they were clustered in the middle levels of qualifications.

These figures suggest that although there was room on TOPS/OJTS both for women who were very well qualified and for women whose previous education was limited, the scheme catered particularly well for women who were 'middle of the road' as far as qualifications were concerned. In no way could it be regarded as a scheme only for the no-hopers, and its public reputation was that of a popular and worthwhile programme to which no stigma attached.

Ethnic minority women
Women from ethnic minorities may have difficulty in obtaining suitable work because of racial discrimination. Even more than women from the dominant white culture, they are concentrated in low skilled, low paid work. Training is therefore especially important for them.

TOPS/OJTS improved the opportunities open to ethnic minority women. More of them found places on the scheme than their numbers in the population as a whole would predict: women of minority ethnic origin formed 3.5 per cent of all economically active women in Great Britain in 1986 but they were 10.7 per cent of female trainees. Even allowing for their greater chance of being unemployed - they comprised 6.5 per cent of all unemployed women - they were still more likely than white women to find a place on TOPS/OJTS.[4] The position with regard to ethnic minority men on TOPS/OJTS was rather different: their representation on the programme (7.8 per cent) was proportional to their representation in the national unemployment figures (7.5 per cent).

Ethnic minority women on TOPS/OJTS were often younger than their white colleagues, with nine out of ten under the age of 35 compared to five out of ten white women trainees. They were also a little less well qualified - 48 per cent had qualifications of O Level standard or higher, compared to 58 per cent of white women on the courses. Somewhat fewer of them had been in work in the month before they started their course (a little under a quarter compared to a third of white women), while those that were not in work had been out of work on average for longer, usually for at least a year, and often for much more.

Miss P. was a young woman in her mid-twenties who lived with her parents in Birmingham. Her father came from the West Indies, but she had been born in England. She had left school at 16 with two CSEs and found work as a packer in a warehouse, but was made redundant from this job in 1979, a year when there were a great many redundancies in the West Midlands. She had been unemployed for nearly seven years when she got a place on a three month catering course leading to City and Guilds Level 1. After finishing the course she was out of work for another ten months, but eventually found work as a catering assistant in an NHS hospital. Although nominally in the catering field, this job involved mainly cleaning and washing up, and she was not able to use the skills she had acquired on her course. After some months she left the hospital to work as a table hand in a small factory.

Miss M., from London, was more fortunate. Like Miss P., she was born in England but her parents came from the West Indies. She was a single mother and had been forced to give up her job as a VDU operator after her child was born, as she found she could not cope with full-time work. She was out of work for six months and 'fed up with being at home'. She found out about the TOPS/OJTS courses at the local Job Centre, and was accepted on a three month course in typing, word processing and business skills. The qualifications she gained enabled her to get a part-time job as a secretary in a hospital, a job with which she expressed herself 'very satisfied'.

Mrs N. had been a teacher in India, but found when she came to England with her two children in 1985 to join her husband that her teaching certificate was not recognised in Britain. After more than a year out of work she retrained in typing, audio-typing and word processing, gaining RSA Stage I qualifications. At the end of the five month course she was still unable to find suitable work, and after several more months spent job hunting she took a job as a sales

37

assistant in a department store. This turned out to be a better move than she had expected, for after four months with the organisation she was promoted to clerical work. She later left the department store to take a clerical job with British Telecom.

Reasons for taking training

As we have seen, women trainees on TOPS/OJTS came from a wide variety of backgrounds in terms of work history, family circumstances and education. With such diverse origins, it is clear that they must have embarked on training with many different purposes in view. For some, training held out the hope of escaping from unemployment; for others, it was the means by which they could rejoin the labour force after a long absence on account of family responsibilities. For those without qualifications in poorly paid and low skilled jobs it offered a way of moving into more desirable work, while for those who already had qualifications and experience which had fallen into disuse, it gave an opportunity to move back up the occupational ladder. For a lot of women training served more than one of these purposes at the same time.

Whatever their specific motive, most women trainees entered their course with very positive attitudes towards training. In the face-to-face interviews which were conducted with trainees, we asked everyone to give in their own words the most important reason why they had decided to go on TOPS/OJTS. In reply, 26 per cent of women referred to their desire to learn new skills, 22 per cent to their intention of returning to a type of work which they had done some years earlier and been forced to give up, and 15 per cent to their wish to increase their knowledge and skills and to improve their confidence. Another 23 per cent wanted to improve their chances of getting a job or escape from unemployment, seven per cent felt that they needed a change of career, and four per cent said they wanted to increase their earnings. Only three per cent said that their main reason for taking training was that other people had advised them to do so. Thus the push to get training came primarily from women's own motivation, and in answer to a further question 83 per cent said that it had been their own idea to get training, and only 17 per cent that it had been suggested by someone else. What is more, this motivation stemmed mainly from an appreciation of the positive gains that training could bring - what we might term 'pull' factors - and the use of training as an alternative to an unsatisfactory present situation was mentioned only by a minority of women.

Many women had been attracted by the idea of getting training for a long time. More than two-fifths said that there had been times before they went on TOPS/OJTS when they definitely would have liked to have taken training or gone back into education, but had not done so. The obstacle which they said had prevented them was in most cases their family commitments, with financial constraints a close second.

For many women, therefore, TOPS/OJTS offered a golden opportunity: the part-time structure of many of the refresher courses was compatible with looking after children and home, there were no fees to be found, and for women training full-time there was a training allowance which, backed by the social security system, enabled them to support their families if need be while they trained. How well did the opportunity live up to its promise? In the next chapter we look at what the courses on which they enrolled were like and explore the nature of the training experience for women.

Notes to Chapter Two
1. Unemployment Unit and Youthaid (1990).
2. In April 1988 the personal allowance for a full-time trainee on OJTS was £38, with an extra £24.70 for a married person whose spouse earned less than £36 net per week; a person claiming unemployment benefit received £32.75 with an extra £20.20 for an adult dependent, provided the dependent did not earn more than that sum.
3. MSC memo 1042/4, June 1986.
4. National figures taken from OPCS Social Survey Division (1987), Table 4.22.

3. The Training Experience

The previous chapter described the many different kinds of women who received off-the-job skills training under TOPS and its successor OJTS. The men on the programme came from an equally wide diversity of backgrounds, and in some ways the programme could be likened to a vocationally orientated Open University, less middle class in ethos than the Open University, but equally giving a second chance to people who, for one reason or another, had missed out the first time round. Two factors were crucial to opening up access to training under TOPS/OJTS to all sorts and conditions of people: first the entry requirements, which were liberal and inclusive rather than restrictive and exclusive, and second the fact that training was free and a subsistence allowance was provided for full-time trainees which was payable as of right and not means-tested.

In accordance with the varied composition of its intake, TOPS/OJTS offered training of a correspondingly wide variety of kinds, and this chapter outlines the range of courses that were available. Drawing on material from the Evaluation Study, it describes the way the courses were run, the qualifications they led to, and the ways in which trainees supported themselves while studying. The last part of the chapter tries to capture the subjective experience of training: it reports the responses to standardised attitude questions about the courses, and quotes the spontaneous comments that women made about the value that training held for them.

The courses
The diversity of courses that could be followed under TOPS/OJTS was enormous. At the one extreme were post-graduate courses in institutions of higher education; such courses were not administered by the Manpower Services Commission, but under certain circumstances course fees could be paid out of TOPS/OJTS funds and the training allowance used to support the trainee while studying. At

the other extreme, but under the same broad TOPS/OJTS umbrella, were courses which trained people for semi-skilled or operative level jobs. These were usually held in government skill centres, which were the late twentieth century descendants of the government training centres that were set up in the First World War; since the demise of TOPS/OJTS they have been privatised. In between was a huge variety of courses for professionals, managers, technicians, white collar office workers and skilled craftsmen and women. Some of these took place in government skill centres, some were specially put on for TOPS/OJTS in colleges of further education and polytechnics, some made use of sponsored places on courses that were already set up, and some were run by profit making private training companies who had been given government contracts.

The courses available under the programme covered all the major occupational groups and no less than 408 distinct skills. The following selection gives some idea of the range of choice: clothing production management; systems analysts; legal executive assistant; travel and tourism clerk; medical secretarial; audio typing for typists; ship surveyor; industrial radiography; handloom weaving; printing plate processing; motor cycle repair and maintenance; precision grinding; plate metal fabrication; domestic appliance servicing; boat building and fitting-out; driving instructor; silver service waiting.

For administrative purposes, these courses were divided into 17 broad training fields, called 'planning groups', and the Evaluation Study covered all but the six smallest of these. The full list of training fields is given in Table 3.1. As the table shows, the six fields that were excluded from the study together accounted for less than eight per cent of trainees.

For the purposes of the Evaluation Study, courses were grouped into three general types. First were those we labelled *technological* courses. These covered the higher level courses in computing skills, together with technician level courses in engineering, science and technology. An eighth of these courses were at managerial, professional and executive level and seven-eighths were at technician level. Roughly two-fifths were held at colleges, two-fifths at private training institutes, and a fifth were held at skill centres. The next group of courses was labelled *clerical and secretarial*. These covered clerical, commercial and general office skills, including training in new office technologies like word processing, together with courses

Table 3.1   Training field of TOPS/OJTS trainees, by sex

	OJTS Evaluation Study Trainees		All TOPS/OJTS trainees
	men %	women %	%
Management	-	-	2
Computer skills	13	6	9
Management services	-	-	1
Clerical/commercial	4	28	13
Shorthand/typing	3	56	25
Engineering science and technology	19	1	10
Making and processing	2	3	2
Automotive	5	*	3
Mechanical engineering	9	*	5
Engineering fabrication	12	*	6
Electrical and electronic engineering	8	*	4
Construction	21	*	11
Driving occupations	-	-	*
Hotel & catering (non-supervisory)	4	4	4
Health, training & welfare	-	-	1
Service & selling	-	-	2
Miscellaneous	-	-	2
Total	100	100	100
(N)	(1,436)	(1,218)	(31,120)

* 0.5% or less, but not zero.

Sources: Columns 1 & 2: Evaluation Study.
Column 3: TOPS/OJTS Follow-Up Survey 1985/86 (own calculations).

Note: Columns 1 and 2 exclude the six smallest training fields in TOPS/OJTS.

in shorthand, typing, and other secretarial skills. Lower level courses in computing skills, such as data preparation, were also classed here. All of these courses were skilled level and three-quarters were college-based, with a quarter run by private training companies. Finally the *manual* group comprised courses in a wide range of skills, including materials processing and repairing; automotive trades; mechanical engineering; engineering fabrication, welding and sheet metal work; electrical and electronic engineering, installation and maintenance; construction; and hotel and catering. Seven-eighths of these were skilled level courses and the rest were operative level. Most manual courses were based at government skill centres.

Skill level of training on TOPS/OJTS compared to ET

Across TOPS/OJTS as a whole (not counting the six small planning groups left out of the Evaluation Study) 20 per cent of trainees were doing technician level training or higher, 76 per cent were training at skilled level, either white or blue collar, and only four per cent were training at operative level. The programme was therefore making a very substantial contribution to Britain's skills needs. In contrast, Employment Training has been accused of making a negligible impact on skills shortages, even by those directly responsible for its administration. The draft Corporate Plan of the Manchester TEC has been reported as saying that ET:

> does not reflect the need for high 'value added' training that equips people who have the capacity with the skills needed now and in the future in the labour market; is overly focussed on the aspirations of the unemployed and takes insufficient account of known or anticipated skill shortages; is funded in a way which encourages low quality, long duration training and fails to provide an incentive for progression or positive outcomes.[1]

It is not possible to make a direct comparison between the skill level of training under TOPS/OJTS and under ET, because the available figures for the two schemes are based on different classification systems that cannot be translated directly one into the other. In addition, information is published for ET only in very broad occupational categories, and, unlike TOPS/OJTS, figures for ET do not distinguish between different skill levels of training. Nevertheless such figures as are available strongly suggest that the range of occupations covered by TOPS/OJTS was much wider than the range currently offered by ET, and that the skill level of training on TOPS/OJTS was on average considerably higher.

The figures for ET are given in Table 3.2. Compared to TOPS/OJTS, there is an almost complete absence of training for higher level occupations. On TOPS/OJTS, computer skills and engineering science and technology were both important training areas, together accounting for 19 per cent of trainees; on ET they are not even big enough to warrant separate classification. A small and valuable corner of more advanced training run on TOPS/OJTS lines does still survive in ET under the name of 'Higher Technology National Training', but in 1989/90 only 7,000 ET trainees out of the year's total of 246,000 (three per cent) received training under this scheme.[2] In contrast, relatively low skill occupations such as 'sales and storage' figure much more importantly on ET than on TOPS/OJTS.

Administrative and clerical training is still important for women on ET, accounting for 53 per cent of places, but the proportion of women training for this type of occupation is considerably smaller than it was on TOPS/OJTS, where a total of 84 per cent trained in the two planning groups clerical/commercial and shorthand/typing. On ET, a new training field has emerged for women: this comprises health, community and personal service occupations which account for 20 per cent of women on ET. Many of these occupations - care assistants and home helps are typical - are low paid and offer poor

Table 3.2   Training occupations of trainees on Employment Training, by sex, 1989/90.

	men %	women %	all %
Administrative and clerical	14	53	26
Creative, & recreational service	4	4	4
Health, community & personal service	4	20	9
Sales & storage	5	4	5
Catering, food preparation & processing	3	4	4
Agricultural & related; fishing	8	2	6
Transport operating	3	*	2
Construction & civil engineering	35	2	25
Electrical & electronic	5	*	3
Mechanical engineering, & metal production & process	5	*	3
Motor vehicle repair & maintenance	5	*	4
Clothing & textiles manufacturing	1	4	2
Other (1% or less each)	7	6	7
Total	100	100	100
(N)	(168,203)	(77,794)	(245,997)

* 0.5% or less, but not zero.

Source: Employment Department (1990a), with additional unpublished details supplied by the Employment Department.

conditions of employment. On TOPS/OJTS less than one per cent of trainees trained in the closest equivalent to this group of occupations, the planning group health, training and welfare.

Training for men on ET is dominated by the construction industry. Thirty-five per cent of all ET places for men are in construction and civil engineering compared to 21 per cent in construction on TOPS/OJTS. As the construction industry is particularly vulnerable in a recession, the prospects of these trainees as we enter 1991 do not seem bright. The other 65 per cent of male trainees on ET are distributed across a range of occupations. Some of these barely figured under TOPS/OJTS, such as agriculture and related occupations (the so-called 'landscape gardeners' and 'conservation workers' of the government schemes of the 1980's - often jobs which involve little more than labouring), and some were much more important under TOPS/OJTS, such as 'mechanical engineering, and metal production and process' for which five per cent of men on ET trained, compared to the 21 per cent on TOPS/OJTS in the nearest comparable group, mechanical engineering and engineering fabrication.

It would be unwise to be too precise about the difference between TOPS/OJTS and ET because of the uncertainties in the statistics. Nevertheless it would be hard to avoid the conclusion that in general TOPS/OJTS aimed to equip trainees with a level of skills that was much higher than the target set by ET.

How the courses were run

TOPS/OJTS courses could last anything from a month to a year. Trainees in the Evaluation Study stayed an average of five months on their course, though the time varied with the subject studied and the level to which it was taken. Refresher courses, for example, could sometimes be quite short. Within a given training field there was a lot of variation in provision and a certain amount of choice, though the choice was greater in large cities than in rural areas. Sometimes trainees, having successfully completed one course, would transfer directly onto another in order to develop their skills to a higher level. Over the country as a whole, the average length of stay on technological and manual courses was six months, and on clerical and secretarial courses it was four months. As a number of the clerical and secretarial courses were part-time, the differences between the three groups in total teaching time was greater than the actual course length indicates.

About eight per cent of trainees went away from home to do their training and were paid a special allowance to cover their board and lodging costs. This was particularly common on the higher level courses, where there was less likely to be a suitable course in the local area. In general, men were much more likely to go away to train than women. The men who did so were on average younger than other men taking part in the programme, and fewer of them had domestic ties.

All TOPS/OJTS courses involved intensive training in classrooms or training workshops. Unlike ET and the Youth Training Scheme, there was no role for work placements with employers, and liaison with employers was minimal. The lack of practical work experience sometimes caused problems for trainees when they left their course, as the following quotations illustrate:

> I have never regretted doing the course. Only that it was not long enough. Nor could it teach you to work at a proper industrial speed. Perhaps it would have been better if at the end of the course the government would have paid trainees for a further 6-12 months! Thereby providing on-the-job training.

> The course I found was very good but however I must mention that I found there wasn't enough practical experience, and I am feeling the results of this now ... more practical is essential.

> I would like to see perhaps employers taking on pupils for a week or two after the course as part of the course.

Trainees on clerical and secretarial courses however rarely complained about the lack of on-the-job training. This was probably because the training they received under TOPS/OJTS followed the traditional model of training for clerical and secretarial jobs, which has always tended to take place in colleges and classrooms, with students gaining their qualifications before they start to look for a job. In contrast, training for manual skills has traditionally been carried out under the apprenticeship system, where trainees are also employees working at the occupation for which they are preparing themselves.

The need to integrate work experience into TOPS/OJTS had periodically come under review and various proposals had been mooted for remedying the situation. One study of skill centre training conducted in the mid-seventies put forward a variety of suggestions about how what it termed 'the gap between training and work' could be bridged.[3] These included improved contacts at a local level between skill centres and employers, and continuing part-time training on a day release basis after the trainee had been placed in a job. An MSC review of the scope and effectiveness of TOPS a year or two later recommended that off-the-job training should be followed by on-the-job training in the workplace, with newly hired trainees continuing to receive the training allowance or part only of the full wage for a short period. Such proposals required careful negotiation with trade unions, who were understandably anxious lest the skilled status of the time-served apprentice be eroded by an influx of trainees from accelerated training programmes - a debate which has been conducted intermittently ever since government training programmes were first introduced in the Great War. In the event, the proposals for integrating off-the-job training with practical work experience were shelved when the deep recession of the early 1980s drew attention away from the refinement of TOPS and focussed it on new programmes to cope with the huge numbers of men and women in the dole queues. The relaunch of TOPS as OJTS was accompanied by an increased emphasis on matching training to market needs, but changes in actual training practice had not gone very far before OJTS itself disappeared from the public scene.

Qualifications gained in training

One outcome which many men and women hope for from adult training is to obtain a recognised qualification which they can show to potential employers. This is particularly important for trainees who do not have previous experience in the field in which they want to work. In fact 62 per cent of TOPS/OJTS trainees in the Evaluation Study said they got a qualification at the end of their course, of which 46 per cent were recognised qualifications awarded by national bodies and 16 per cent were course completion certificates or qualifications awarded by the organisation running the course. The former were generally much more valued by trainees, as they felt they carried considerably more weight with employers. The chances of obtaining a recognised qualification depended on whether one was offered on the course, and such qualifications were more often available on the longer courses. Older trainees were almost as successful as their younger colleagues, and trainees with no previous qualifications were nearly as successful as those who already had good educational credentials.

Rather more women trainees succeeded in obtaining a recognised qualification than men (51 per cent of women versus 42 per cent of men). This was because of their concentration on clerical and secretarial courses, which more commonly led to such qualifications. In all, 46 per cent of women trainees who had no previous educational qualifications acquired their first recognised qualifications on TOPS/OJTS, while 65 per cent of previously unqualified women gained a qualification of some kind.

Once more, it is not easy to make comparisons between TOPS/OJTS and ET. It has been officially reported that 34 per cent of men on ET and 42 per cent of women 'worked towards' a qualification, with success rates of 56 per cent each.[4] A simple calculation yields the figures of 19 per cent of men and 23 per cent of women leaving ET with a qualification, and Table 3.3 sets these figures alongside the corresponding percentages for TOPS/OJTS. However the ET figures cover all trainees who leave the scheme, whereas the figures for TOPS/OJTS refer only to those who completed their courses, a difference which is bound to bias the results in favour of TOPS/OJTS. On the other hand, the ET figures include individual credits which can be accumulated over a period of time towards qualifications such as those awarded by the BTEC, whereas the figures for TOPS/OJTS only count qualifications which have been fully completed. In view of these differences, it is impossible to attach a precise value to the difference between the two schemes in the proportion of trainees gaining qualifications, though it would be hard to resist the conclusion that many more did so on TOPS/OJTS than on ET.

The published figures for qualifications gained on ET do not distinguish between recognised qualifications and qualifications granted by the particular organisation running the course, such as course completion certificates. Since ET was launched, there has been substantial progress towards the standardisation of vocational qualifications through the framework of the National Council for Vocational Qualifications. Though the principal of standardisation has been generally welcomed, there has been criticism of the particular way in which it has been implemented, with some commentators arguing that standards have been set too low and that it is wrong to

Table 3.3 **Comparison between the qualifications gained by TOPS/OJTS trainees and trainees on Employment Training**

| | TOPS/OJTS (completers only) (1986) | | ET (all leavers) (July 89-March 90) | |
	men %	women %	men %	women %
all gaining a qualification	57	67	19	23
of which:				
recognised	42	51	-	-
not recognised	16	16	-	-
(Base N)	(372)	(318)	(299,845)	(161,455)

Sources: Columns 1 & 2: Evaluation Study.
　　　　 Column 3: Employment Department (1990a) (own calculations).

Note:　ET figures include credits towards a qualification; these are not counted in the figures for TOPS/OJTS.

have the same people who train the candidate also responsible for carrying out assessments.[5] The framework of National Vocational Qualifications was not in place in 1986, but the qualifications of TOPS/OJTS trainees were classed as 'recognised' only if they were awarded by established examining and validating bodies, such as City and Guilds and the Royal Society of Arts, or by professional bodies responsible for setting, maintaining and examining standards in their field of competence, such as the Institute of Chartered Accountants.

Financial support
All full-time trainees on TOPS/OJTS were entitled to a training allowance. The allowance was large enough to cover basic living costs other than housing: in April 1988 it was worth £38 per week or £62.70 if the trainee was married. In appropriate circumstances it could be topped up by housing benefit or supplementary benefit. In the Evaluation Study, 19 per cent of women trainees who drew the training allowance received social security benefits as well (not counting child benefit). Fifty-seven per cent of women trainees who got the training allowance relied for additional support on their

partner's earnings, while 16 per cent drew on their savings or redundancy payments and five per cent took on casual or part-time work at evenings and weekends.

The third of women trainees who trained part-time and so were not eligible for the training allowance relied more heavily on other sources of income. Once more, the mainstay for many was their partner's earnings: 71 per cent quoted this as a source of income while they were in training. However 29 per cent received state benefits, 21 per cent drew on their savings or past redundancy payments, and 12 per cent had a part-time or casual job.

Financial back-up to their training was important to the women in the study, and in no way could be dismissed as just pin money. Twenty-three per cent of women trainees were single, 13 per cent had marriages which had broken up, and some were widows. In addition five per cent, though married, had a husband who was out of work at the time they started their training through unemployment, sickness or retirement. In all, more than two-fifths of women trainees were the main breadwinners in their household, and two-fifths of these - 17 per cent of all women trainees - had dependent children to provide for. These women would have found it very difficult to take training had the financial arrangements been less favourable. As it was, 14 per cent of women who were the main breadwinners suffered what they described as a 'large drop' in their living standards as a result of going on the course, and a further 20 per cent experienced a 'small drop'. Fifteen per cent of women breadwinners actually went into debt.

The training allowance was not as vital for women who had a partner who was earning unless their partner's wages were very low, but it gave them financial independence and was a mark of the importance that society attached to their new skills. It undoubtedly was an encouragement to train. Even so, women with partners in work could also find their living standards somewhat reduced if they gave up a job in order to train: 14 per cent of women who had partners in work experienced a small drop in living standards when they went on their course and two per cent felt a large drop; five per cent went into debt.

The financial position of women on TOPS/OJTS was in general considerably more advantageous than it is on ET. On ET the £10 training allowance may be all that they receive in their own name, and this sum can easily be consumed by the extra costs entailed by taking part in the programme. The one respect in which the financial provisions of ET are more generous is in the contribution that is made to the child care costs of lone parents, though places for women eligible for such payments have been vulnerable to recent cuts in the government budget for training.

Satisfaction with the training experience

The women who took part in the Evaluation Study expressed a high level of satisfaction with their experience of adult training. More than four-fifths said they were either 'very satisfied' or 'fairly satisfied' with the content of the training provided, the support and help they got from teachers, the relevance of the course to their employment prospects, and the value of the course to their personal development, and on all these counts the 'very satisfied's' easily outnumbered those who were only 'fairly satisfied'. Though most male trainees were also well pleased, the level of satisfaction was higher for women than for men.

When they filled in their questionnaires for the postal follow-up in spring 1989, a very large number of women added comments describing the way in which their training had contributed to their own personal development. Personal gains included the ability to act decisively, increased motivation, and the satisfaction of having achieved something worthwhile. However the benefit that was most often stressed by women (though rarely mentioned by men) was that training gave them confidence in themselves. This was a key factor, particularly for women whose daily lives had for many years been spent at home with children. The following quotations illustrate the way that many felt:

> This course gave me the confidence to return to full-time work.

> Invaluable to a person who needs an up-date on office procedure and equipment - which results in an assertiveness and confidence building. How else can you gain experience when you've not worked for some 12 years with no financial resources yourself to pay for a course?

> I find I am often drawing from information and experience gained on the course which, in turn, has increased my confidence not only in my job but generally as well.

> The course helped considerably in rebuilding confidence and gave me a head-start with employers who have all been impressed with course content on CV.

> My deepest thanks for the opportunity. Truly fantastic. Just what I needed after 19 years at home ... I would not have easily faced returning to work without the knowledge it gave me, confidence in former abilities, skills it refreshed, stimulus it provided, update and practical application of modern technological equipment and development, and a basic knowledge and practice on computers.

For these women, the training experience was undoubtedly a good one.

Notes to Chapter Three

1. *Corporate Plan Structure*, Manchester TEC 1990, Part 1, Section 4, quoted in Unemployment Unit and Youthaid (1991). The funding mechanisms for ET have since been revised in order to reward schemes which produce positive outcomes in terms of the number of trainees gaining qualifications and/or jobs.
2. Wilson (1990).
3. Berthoud (1978).
4. Employment Department (1990a).
5. See, for example, Prais, S. (1989).

4. Segregation in Training

TOPS/OJTS gave opportunities to many women which would otherwise have been closed to them, and they were only slightly outnumbered by men on the programme. However, though all TOPS/OJTS courses were in principle open on equal terms to men and women, in reality the training that was offered was highly segregated by gender. Most women trained on courses where there were very few men, and most men trained on courses where there were hardly any women at all. In this the programme was but a mirror image of the labour market in the world outside.

TOPS/OJTS was in no way unusual in this respect; gender divisions in training are very pronounced in the government's Youth Training programmes and, as we have seen in the last chapter, appear to be equally persistent in Employment Training.[1] Nevertheless, a very small number of women did train in subjects that are not traditionally regarded as suitable for females, and the experiences and subsequent progress of these women are of particular interest.

The job market in Britain is also segregated to a very significant degree by ethnic origin. Although ethnic minority women were well represented on TOPS/OJTS in numerical terms, we need to enquire whether there was any racial segregation within the programme. This issue is dealt with in the last part of the chapter.

Gendered training
Thirty-one per cent of male trainees in the Evaluation Study did courses classed in the technological group, seven per cent did clerical and secretarial courses, and 62 per cent did manual courses. For women, the corresponding proportions were five per cent, 88 per cent, and seven per cent. Nine out of ten trainees on clerical and secretarial courses were women, and nine out of ten trainees on technological and manual courses were men. In crude terms, this was the extent of segregation by sex within TOPS/OJTS.

Table 3.1 in the last chapter, based on the large national sample of trainees for whom we had administrative data, has already indicated how unequal the sex balance was on many courses. While male trainees were distributed across a wide range of occupations, forming more than half of trainees in eight broad subject areas or 'planning groups', women were very heavily concentrated in a restricted number of occupations, forming the majority of trainees in only three. Indeed, in six planning groups women constituted less than five per cent of trainees. Only in two planning groups - making and processing and non-supervisory hotel and catering work - was there anything approaching an equal balance between the sexes. In the third most evenly balanced group, computer skills, women were outnumbered by men by nearly three to one.

Striking as they are, these figures do not reveal the full extent of segregation. The finer the distinctions that are made between courses and the greater the detail in which one examines the picture, the bigger the contrast appears between the training that men were doing and the training done by women. In the Evaluation Study's interview sample of 785 trainees, 16 women had done courses classified under the 'computer skills' planning group. According to their own description, five of these women had actually taken courses in word processing and business skills, doing training to prepare them for secretarial or clerical work, leaving only eleven women who had studied programming, systems analysis or computer operating.

A further illustration of the illusory nature of the integration of training for men and women is found in the making and processing planning group, which at first sight appeared to have well balanced numbers of male and female trainees. Of the 13 women in the study who trained in this planning group, eleven were in fact learning sewing machining. This was officially classed as operative level work rather than skilled level, and was done by very few men. In fact analysis of the recent history of the clothing industry has suggested that sewing machining is classed as semi-skilled work precisely because it is usually done by women.[2] The remaining two women in the 'making and processing' planning group were training in basic printed circuit board assembly. This was a job in which there were equal numbers of male and female trainees, but, like sewing machining, it was classed as operative level.

The remaining planning group which involved roughly equal numbers of men and women was catering, where about a quarter of trainees were on operative level courses. Here at least there seemed to be a degree of equality between the sexes, for there was no evidence that in catering women trainees were any less likely than men to be on skilled level courses. For the rest, however, it was a different story. Amongst all the 377 women in the Evaluation Study only four had enrolled on technician level courses in the planning group 'engineering science and technology', and only three had penetrated the traditionally masculine skilled manual crafts.

On the other side of the gender equation, there were 22 men on clerical and secretarial courses. Fifteen of these trained for clerical occupations including accountancy, and two trained in data preparation and calculating machine operating, leaving only five who trained in the conventionally feminine secretarial skills of shorthand and typing. Two of these five men were registered disabled.

One obvious result of the segregation between men and women within TOPS/OJTS was that many fewer women than men trained on higher level courses. In the larger sample of trainees for whom we had administrative data, 32 per cent of men were training at technician level or higher, compared to only six per cent of women.

Women in a man's world: engineering science and technology

It takes some unusual qualities on the part of a woman to train for a job which is nearly always done by a man. The women in the present study who did this were few in number and it would be risky to generalise about them, but it is fascinating to study their individual histories and see what led them down this road.

All four women who enrolled on courses in engineering science and technology were already well qualified before they began. Two had degrees in scientific subjects, one had a Higher National Certificate, and the fourth had A Levels. Two had been born abroad in countries where it was less unusual for women to do this kind of work, and had settled in Britain as adults. None of the four had any children, and all were in their thirties or very early forties. Their attempts to get a foothold in a man's world met with mixed success.

Ms L. was one who benefited a lot from her course. She had held a variety of short term jobs in her native country, and when she settled in Britain had decided to go back to college to study for A Levels.

This was followed by another spell abroad, but on her return to Britain her marriage broke up and she found herself needing a job. After searching for work for some months without success she decided that she needed further training 'to get useful skills that were recognised, as I couldn't get work to utilise the skills I had'. She applied for a course in electro-mechanical draughtsmanship, a new departure for her, and had to wait more than six months for a place. The course lasted seven months, and although it did not lead to a formal qualification she was nonetheless able to find work almost immediately afterwards as an architectural draughtsman for a large national construction company. A year later she was promoted within the same firm to do 'computer-aided drawing, printing, etc., with responsibility for specific projects'. Although this was not exactly the field she had trained in, she nevertheless found her course extremely useful:

> The course was useful for the skills it gave me rather than the specific knowledge about electro-mechanics. As it happens, I found myself working for the building trade (and maybe Architectural Drawing would have been a more relevant course, had it existed), but the general rules of drawing, drawing office procedures, CAD operation etc. seem to apply for all disciplines.

Miss E., a geography graduate, was also well pleased with her training. She had left teaching in order to turn what had initially been a part-time interest in gardening into a career, and her course as a horticultural technician enabled her to progress further:

> The course was an excellent basic retraining... All the people at the college I was at who were on an MSC training grant greatly appreciated the opportunity of retraining.

She eventually became a garden designer, working at what might be perceived to be the 'feminine' end of the spectrum of technology.

The other two women who enrolled for courses in engineering science and technology failed to complete their training, though for very different reasons. Mrs F. already had a degree in mechanical engineering from an Eastern European university, but had only been able to get short-term contract work since settling in this country. She felt that her career was impeded by her lack of familiarity with computer applications in her field, and so applied for a course in computer assisted design and manufacture. Unfortunately the course did not match up to her expectations, proving to be too low level for her needs. After leaving she continued to look for a more suitable course, but said, 'I have not been able to find a course that teaches what I need to know for my job in sufficient depth'.

Mrs R. dropped out of her course not because it was unsuitable, but because of sheer bad luck. Despite a strong scientific background she had been working for many years well below her potential, taking, as she put it, 'any job that suited my husband'. After her marriage broke up she decided to retrain in electronics. By an oversight she was notified late of the start of the course, and as a result she missed the first two weeks and found herself unable to catch up. Her difficulties were compounded by the fact that her course was held some fifty miles from where she lived, and there was a lack of accommodation locally, which meant she had to commute long distances each day. Her health suffered under the strain of this, and she eventually withdrew.

One factor which clearly impeded the possibility of women training in engineering science and technology was their lack of work experience on the lower rungs of these professions. All four women in the present study who enrolled on such courses were already educated to a high standard; none had come up through the ranks of industry. The men on courses in engineering science and technology often came from a different background: though three-fifths of them had A Levels or higher qualifications, two-fifths were without qualifications of this standard. However, the large majority of these less well qualified men had previous industrial experience in jobs related to the field in which they wished to train. As examples we could cite an electrical service engineer who took a course in robotics, a turner and capstan setter/operator who trained in computer numerical control programming and operating, and an air conditioning engineer who retrained as a service mechanic for computers. The routes via which these men had reached their technician level training in engineering were largely closed to women, because for the most part women were excluded from the craft apprenticeships which were the starting point.

Women in computing

Computing is a new and expanding field and women have found it easier to establish a foothold there than in engineering. Many of the women who did clerical and secretarial courses on TOPS/OJTS learned to use computers for word processing or accounts, and others whose courses fell into the 'computing skills' planning group studied data preparation or gained a basic appreciation of information technology. Eleven women in the Evaluation Study took courses in higher level computer skills, mainly computer programming and systems analysis, and women formed around a quarter of all trainees on courses of this type. They resembled the four women who took technician level courses in engineering science and technology in several respects: they were relatively young (no-one was over 40), most were childless (only three of the eleven had children), and they were well qualified (all but three had been educated to A Level standard, and four were graduates). Some of them had already had experience of computing, or had a background in mathematics or science, but the majority did not. At the end of their training, seven of the eleven succeeded in getting work which used the skills they had acquired.

Undoubtedly there were career opportunities for women who took computing courses, though some relevant previous experience was helpful, both in coping with the work demanded on the course and in securing appropriate employment afterwards. The case of Ms A., a single woman in her late twenties, illustrates this. She had decided some time previously that computing was the career for her. She already had a degree but had lived abroad for several years after she graduated. On her return to England she did a college course which led to a City and Guilds Part III qualification in programming, but in Liverpool where she lived jobs were hard to come by and she was unemployed for three months. A second course, this time on TOPS/OJTS, enabled her to progress to systems analysis, and on completing this she managed to get a job as a computing technician with an insurance company.

However, computing is a field where natural aptitude counts for a lot, and if this was present, it was possible to do well despite the lack of any previous experience. Mrs R. clearly had this aptitude. She possessed both A Levels and secretarial qualifications and had held a series of clerical and secretarial posts. Despite her qualifications, she described her main tasks in her last job as 'typing, filing, telephone, organising trips'. Not surprisingly, she became dissatisfied with her career, and applied for a training course because 'I wanted to further myself and realise my full potential'. Her course in Business Computing, which she had to wait more than six months to get a place on, secured her a job as a programmer with a local authority. She later left this to join a small software house where her work involved 'developing fourth generation applications on IBM mainframes'. Both jobs she found far more satisfying than her previous secretarial work.

Though it was possible to do well in computing without previous experience, certain personal characteristics did appear to be important for success. There were one or two exceptions, but nearly all the women who went on to follow a career in computing after their TOPS/OJTS course were young, had a good educational background, and had no young children to care for. Those who managed to stay in the field without having all these factors on their side obtained work at a somewhat lower level. Miss H., for example, had left school at 15 without any qualifications, and had worked for several years in retailing. She was bored by this and wanted a new career, and after a year out of work got a place on a course in 'Understanding Information Technology'. She went straight from this to a job as a senior computer operator in a large private company.

More usually, however, the obstacles presented by having young children or lacking educational qualifications proved too great to enable women to compete in the high tech world of computing. Mrs D., for example, was a divorcee with two young children. She had started her course in the hope of getting a better paid job, but was forced to give it up because of the difficulty of finding and paying for a child minder. Mrs W. had only CSE qualifications, and found her course in business computing too difficult. As she explained,

> I had been out of education for 16 years - I found the course seemed to be aimed at people who had A Level and degree qualifications and I have neither. I left the course three weeks early due to a serious illness partly caused by the hard work I was putting in trying to make sense of things.

In contrast to the women, there were quite a lot of men who went on higher level TOPS/OJTS computing courses without having particularly good educational qualifications. Two-fifths of male trainees on such courses had qualifications below A Level standard, and well over half of these less well qualified men had no work experience which could be deemed relevant to their course. However nearly all of these men were very young, in their twenties or early thirties. Men without either good academic qualifications or previous relevant experience had less success in pursuing a career in computing after the end of their course than did better qualified men, but even so, around half succeeded in finding work which used their new skills.

If it was possible for relatively unqualified and inexperienced men to be launched on a career in computing by TOPS/OJTS, it has to be asked why so few women in similar circumstances made the attempt. The Evaluation Study looked only at people who had obtained places on TOPS/OJTS courses and we have no information about people who had applied and been turned away, but from what we know about the way the scheme was run it seems unlikely that there was any systematic bias against women in the selection process or that disproportionately more women than men had their applications rejected. Across the TOPS/OJTS programme as a whole there was virtually no difference between the proportion of men and the proportion of women who said that the course they did was their first choice (87 per cent of men, 86 per cent of women). What, then, discouraged women from training in computing skills?

Part of the answer may lie in many women's lack of confidence in their own abilities: some women may simply not think big enough when it comes to their own future. In addition, there is a common conception that logical thinking is not a feminine attribute, and many women are frightened of mathematical concepts, which are important in computing. The fact that women trainees were on average older than men may also have counted against them: nearly all the men who enrolled on computing courses without previous relevant experience or good educational qualifications were under 35. Women in their twenties and early thirties are often too busy raising their families to think about training in a new field. By the time they are ready to plan their return to work, women who might have had an aptitude for computing may consider themselves - or be considered by others - to be too old.

Traditional masculine crafts

So far we have described women who were taking relatively high level training to enter the masculine world of the new technologies, where there was a big and growing demand for highly skilled labour, and where good educational qualifications could act as an entry ticket. In such jobs attitudes towards women might be expected to be less rigid, for they do not carry the weight of a long tradition in which women have played no part. What, then, about the women who sought skilled level training in the older trades where training was traditionally apprenticeship based, where educational qualifications counted for less, and where there was a long-standing masculine work culture?

Unfortunately the Evaluation Study can add very little to our understanding of the experiences of such women. Outside of the catering trade, where trainees were recruited equally from amongst men and women, hardly any women embarked on TOPS/OJTS courses in skilled manual crafts. The manual courses that numbered more than a miniscule proportion of women among their students - notably sewing machining and printed circuit board assembly - were classed not as skilled, but as operative level courses. In the larger sample of TOPS/OJTS trainees for whom administrative data were analysed there were only 17 out of over twelve hundred women trainees - a mere 1.4 per cent - who took courses in any of the five planning groups covering manual occupations where most courses were classed as skilled level. These planning groups were automotive trades, mechanical engineering, engineering fabrication, electrical and electronic engineering, and construction. Indeed, automotive trades, engineering fabrication and construction boasted but one woman trainee each. In the interview sample of 785 trainees there was a grand total of three women trainees in these five occupational groups. All of these three women were in their mid-twenties and had no children, and all trained in electrical or electronic work, rather than the older crafts which also tended to be heavier and dirtier.

We have met one of these women already in Chapter Two. Mrs V. had worked for several years as a sewing machinist until a move to a new town reduced her chances of getting a decent job. She was encouraged by the number of electronics factories near her new home to enrol on a short skill centre course in basic electronics, which she completed successfully. She had no difficulty finding work afterwards, and in fact changed jobs twice to take a better job when the opportunity arose. The job she was doing when we last contacted her, some two years after the end of the course, was with a leading company in a very high tech field. She described her tasks there as 'assembling chassis and board together; some soldering - even training some of the new people in soldering; stripping wires and a few odd things'. Her new skills enabled her to earn the kind of wages that normally only men can get:

> Without the course I went on, I don't think I would ever earn that much in a month. For example, if I did stay in sewing I would probably earn between £250 and £400 (if I work really *hard*), but now it's £550 plus.

The future also looked bright:

> One thing I forgot to mention is that I might take another course in September...if the firm can get me on, as they think I can do better, and I might end up in a test department. It's because they know I've got my certificate in Basic Electronics.

Miss L. enrolled on a course as a sewing machine mechanic (though sewing machinists are nearly always women, the machines they use are usually serviced and repaired by men). Being unemployed at the time, she said she had hoped to gain:

> a new skill - something different. I have had a go at everything else. I thought it was an unusual course to take for a girl.

She found the course 'very stimulating', but did not complete it because of ill health. As a result she did not feel she knew enough to apply for a job as a mechanic, and she returned to her former employment in the catering trade.

Miss T. had a similarly adventurous spirit, though it took some perseverance to get the training she wanted. She had seven O Levels, but had worked only in low grade clerical and shop assistant jobs:

> I wanted a skill. I was in a dead-end job, and I wanted a career. I saw the course in the Job Centre.

The course was in electrical installation and maintenance, but she did not get a place immediately:

> I applied in (town A) first who didn't seem to know what was going on. Then I applied again in (town B), who were terrific. It was eleven months in all (between first applying and starting on the course).

The first part of her course was held in her home town, but the second part took place some distance away, and she moved into lodgings in order to attend. She stayed in training for seven months in total, and gained both Part I and Part II of the City and Guilds examinations. After qualifying, she thought about doing further training in the WRAF, but was put off by the length of commitment required and by the discipline. This delayed her search for work, but she eventually got a job with a small specialist firm, fitting electronic alarm systems in buses.

These three women were unusually determined in that they were willing to be solitary females on all male courses. Yet like the women on technological courses they too were hoping to take advantage of opportunities opening up in new and growing industries, rather than trying to break down barriers against women in old established crafts. The fact that so many of the women training in predominantly masculine fields were young and without children was undoubtedly no coincidence. The lack of family ties may well have encouraged an adventurous spirit, but it also made it easier for them to envisage embarking on careers where full-time work is the norm and few concessions are made to family commitments.

Racial segregation

Chapter Two showed how women of minority ethnic origin were over-represented on TOPS/OJTS courses, both in relation to their numbers in the working population as a whole, and in relation to their numbers amongst the unemployed. In the wider labour market, ethnic minority women in Britain tend to be concentrated at the bottom end of the occupational scale, especially in low skilled, low paid service jobs such as cleaning or kitchen work, and in semi-skilled jobs in manufacturing industry.[3] In TOPS/OJTS, although ethnic minority women were found on all types of courses where women had more than a negligible presence, they were still over-represented in the 'making and processing' planning group, and on non-supervisory hotel and catering courses. The relevant figures are given in part (a) of Table 4.1.

These differences in the ethnic composition of the various planning groups tended to coincide with differences in the average skill level of the training, with the result shown in Table 4.2(a) that ethnic minority women formed nine per cent of women training at technician level or higher, ten per cent of women training at skilled level, but 19 per cent of women training at operative level. For male trainees there was a similar association between minority ethnic origin and a lower skill level of training, as part (b) of the same table demonstrates.

However segregation by ethnic origin on TOPS/OJTS was not only observable in variations in the skill level of training. We have already described how men on TOPS/OJTS did a much more varied range of courses than women, and one concomitant of this was that

Table 4.1   Ethnic balance in training fields on TOPS/OJTS, by sex

	white %	minority ethnic origin %	Total %	Base N
(a) Women				
Computer skills	92	8	100	(75)
Clerical/commercial	92	8	100	(345)
Shorthand/typing	89	11	100	(676)
Engineering science and technology	(5)	(3)	-	(8)
Making and processing	(34)	(6)	-	(40)
Automotive	(1)	(0)	-	(1)
Mechanical engineering	(5)	(1)	-	(6)
Engineering fabrication	(1)	(0)	-	(1)
Electrical and electronic engineering	(3)	(3)	-	(6)
Construction	(3)	(0)	-	(3)
Hotel & catering (non-supervisory)	86	14	100	(50)
(b) Men				
Computer skills	92	8	100	(192)
Clerical/commercial	86	14	100	(55)
Shorthand/typing	(31)	(2)	-	(37)
Engineering science and technology	93	7	100	(276)
Making and processing	(31)	(2)	-	(33)
Automotive	93	7	100	(75)
Mechanical engineering	88	12	100	(137)
Engineering fabrication	97	3	100	(171)
Electrical and electronic engineering	86	14	100	(123)
Construction	95	5	100	(313)
Hotel & catering (non-supervisory)	98	2	100	(56)

Source: Evaluation Study seven per cent sample of trainees from registration data.

Note: Where the base number is less than 50, sample numbers are reported instead of percentages.

Table 4.2   Skill level of TOPS/OJTS course, by ethnic origin and sex

	white %	minority ethnic origin %	Total %	Base N
(a) Women				
technician level or higher	91	9	100	(76)
skilled level	90	10	100	(1,072)
operative level	81	19	100	(59)
(b) Men				
technician level or higher	92	8	100	(460)
skilled level	93	7	100	(949)
operative level	83	17	100	(53)

Source: Evaluation Study seven per cent sample of trainees from
        registration data.

for men there was also quite marked ethnic segregation between courses offering training at the same skill level but for different occupations. This is apparent in Table 4.1(b). Men from ethnic minorities formed only three per cent of trainees in engineering fabrication and five per cent in construction, but they constituted 12 per cent of trainees in mechanical engineering and 14 per cent in electrical and electronic engineering. It was perhaps no coincidence that this last group of occupations, which seemed to offer the best opportunities to women who wanted to break into traditionally masculine occupations, also offered the best opportunities for skilled manual training to men from minority ethnic groups.

If we are to be sure that all opportunities are open equally to men and women regardless of their colour or culture, then the processes which generate the concentration of ethnic minority trainees on certain courses need to be understood. One explanation to consider is that ethnic minority trainees did not have the qualifications needed for entry to the higher level courses. If this were true, it would not explain segregation between training courses for occupations classed as the same skill level, but it could explain the over-representation of ethnic minority men and women on less skilled courses.

It is not easy to test this hypothesis because the larger sample of trainees for whom administrative data were analysed did not include information on qualifications, for these were not recorded as part of the normal administrative process. Information on qualifications was collected for the smaller interview sample, but in this sample the total number of people belonging to ethnic minorities who did courses either at technician level or higher or at operative level was very small. However, the proportion of men and women from ethnic minorities who had no educational qualifications at all (22 per cent) was very similar to the proportion of white trainees with no qualifications (23 per cent). The same was true for female trainees on skilled level courses: 22 per cent of white women and 22 per cent of ethnic minority women on such courses had no educational qualifications.

One noticeable contrast however between white and ethnic minority trainees was the proportion of the latter who had studied abroad; around a fifth of ethnic minority women and a similar proportion of ethnic minority men had gained all their educational qualifications overseas. It is difficult to assess the standard of foreign qualifications in relation to British standards, but, superficially at least, most of the foreign qualifications that trainees possessed seemed to be equivalent at least to O Level GCE and most appeared to be somewhat higher than this. One reason why ethnic minority women were over-represented on lower level courses may therefore be that the selection process for entry to higher level courses did not give sufficient weight to the qualifications they had gained abroad.[4]

Another possible explanation of the clustering of ethnic minority men and women on courses for certain occupations is the existence of direct racial discrimination, such that ethnic minority trainees were more likely than whites to be refused places on certain courses which they applied for. There is however no evidence in the Evaluation Study to suggest that direct discrimination of this type took place, for there was very little difference between whites and ethnic minority trainees in the proportion saying that the course they did was not their first choice. Fourteen per cent of white women had not got their first choice, compared to 16 per cent of ethnic minority women, and 13 per cent of white men had failed to get their first choice compared to 12 per cent of ethnic minority men - differences which, with the small numbers of ethnic minority trainees involved, mean very little indeed. Further counter-evidence for the hypothesis of direct discrimination is provided by the fact that ethnic minority trainees waited on average rather less time than whites to get a place on the course they chose, a pattern which held true for both men and women.

The mechanisms which combine to create any form of social segregation, whether by class, gender or race, are complex, and are not always obvious or intentional. The Evaluation Study failed to capture those that influenced the allocation of ethnic minority trainees to TOPS/OJTS courses. The most likely explanation of the segregation that existed may be that in choosing which course to do, ethnic minority trainees were guided by a realistic assessment of the pattern of discrimination and opportunity in the labour market outside TOPS/OJTS. Whatever its causes, it is important to acknowledge that a degree of segregation did exist, as facing the facts is the first step towards tackling the problem.

At the same time the extent of racial segregation on TOPS/OJTS should not be exaggerated. It is very difficult to get an accurate picture of the extent of racial segregation on current government training programmes, whether for young people or for adults, but the evidence suggests that when training programmes rely heavily on placements with employers, such as Youth Training or Employment Training, then the potential for racial discrimination in training is greatly increased. It is not uncommon for employers to refuse to accept black trainees for certain types of work, and yet, despite anti-racist guidelines intended to prevent such practices, these employers continue to be allocated trainees simply because the pressure to find placements for large numbers of trainees is so great.[5] Though racial segregation on TOPS/OJTS undoubtedly existed, it is probably fair to say that its extent was considerably less than on programmes where training is constructed around practical work placements. Viewed in this light, the issue touches on yet another aspect of the debate between the merits of a training scheme which provides centrally planned off-the-job training, and a scheme which is primarily geared to the demands of local employers.

Notes to Chapter Four
1. An analysis of the gendered nature of training within the Youth Training Scheme is given by C. Cockburn (1987).
2. See, for example, A. Coyle (1982).
3. Brown, C. (1984).

4. The Evaluation Study did not collect information on language difficulties, which may also have been a factor in the over-representation of ethnic minority men and women on lower level courses.

5. E. de Sousa (1989) lists 28 large national companies together providing places for nearly 7,000 YTS trainees in October 1987 who between them had a grand total of 34 blacks on the scheme.

5. Finding Work

One particularly influential idea in the original conception of TOPS/OJTS was what was termed in the jargon of the time 'training for stock'. Employers train people to do a particular job in a particular organisation at a particular time; TOPS/OJTS was set up to train people not for specific jobs that were earmarked for them, but in order to form a pool of skilled labour that could be drawn on by the economy as a whole. Furthermore, it was believed that careful analysis of economic and industrial trends would enable future skills needs to be anticipated, so that the opportunities presented by technological development could be exploited without delay. In particular, by keeping a high level of investment in training during periods of recession, when training activities by employers tend to be reduced, it was hoped to put an end to the recurrent skills shortages which had plagued the economy during the 'stop-go' years. This was known as training 'counter-cyclically'. These ideas, which stress the importance of centralised planning and public investment, were clearly at variance with the central tenets of Thatcherism and with the Thatcherite belief in the responsibility and ability of the market to provide the skills that Britain needed.

The popularity of TOPS/OJTS, particularly for women, was never doubted, but nevertheless funds were steadily withdrawn from the programme and it disappeared finally with the launch of Employment Training in 1988. It was not only the interventionist nature of the programme that ensured its downfall. Place for place, TOPS/OJTS was expensive compared to ET, because of the training allowance and because training took place off-the-job. What is more, the government took the view that 'training for stock' was wasteful and inefficient.

The role of evaluation
The TOPS/OJTS model of adult training had been developed over a lengthy period, building on arrangements which had originated in the

early years of the century and had been periodically reviewed and updated. Its abandonment in favour of a quite different model of adult training was strongly influenced by market ideology, and it is one of the contentions of this book that the charge that it was ineffective and too expensive was not based on adequate evidence. The Evaluation Study was set in motion when policy changes were already underway, and its evidence came too late to be taken into consideration before the scheme was closed down. This evidence was that it had given an opportunity which was of real use to many kinds of people, and which was particularly valued by women. Good skills training is bound to be expensive, whoever pays for it; the claim that TOPS/OJTS was too expensive is valid only if the returns in terms of the kinds of skilled labour needed by the economy were disproportionately small. Nor was the wastefulness of training for stock self-evident; on the contrary, this is a testable hypothesis, whose verification depends on the long-term destinations of trainees.

Although it is now gaining ground, the role of formal evaluation in the evolution of public policy has been under-developed in Britain, particularly when compared to its prominence in North America. Any large scale policy impinges on the world in many different ways, and its proper evaluation is correspondingly complex. This does not mean that it should not be attempted, but evaluation is made particularly difficult when new policies are introduced and replaced at great speed. Training policy in the eighties has been characterised by continual changes of direction and control.

Evaluation of TOPS/OJTS has to take into account many different aspects of the programme. As well as direct measures of costs and output (namely, skilled labour), it is also relevant to consider the kinds of people the programme embraced and the people who were excluded, the nature of the training experience, the extent and causes of drop-out, and whether the programme had any indirect and unintended effects, such as encouraging employers to reduce their own investment in training. Most of all it is important to examine whether the programme was of any long term benefit to the people who took part in it. The Evaluation Study explored only some of these issues, but despite this, it taught us a lot more than was known before about the value of adult skills training.

Monitoring placement rates

When TOPS was launched in the seventies, the Manpower Services Commission set up a system of regular monitoring which at the time represented a considerable step forward in the production of information to assist the development of policy. Each quarter a follow-up survey was conducted of a one in six sample of trainees, using postal questionnaires sent out three months after they had completed their training. The information collected through these questionnaires was used to calculate two measures to which a good deal of attention was paid: the proportion of trainees who found work following their course, which was known as the 'placement rate', and the proportion who found work using the skills in which they had trained - in training jargon, the 'in trade' placement rate. It was suspected that three months might in some cases be too short a period to give a fair indication of the number of trainees who would eventually find work, but the choice of this interval was a compromise with the need to ensure that training provision matched market needs. With prompt feedback, courses which were unsuccessful in getting trainees into jobs could be modified or closed, and fields where trainees were proving very successful could be expanded. This series of surveys was continued without interruption when TOPS was relaunched as OJTS in 1985, right up until the demise of OJTS in 1988.

Results from these surveys aggregated for men and women are plotted in Figure 5.1 from the beginning of 1980 right up until the demise of TOPS/OJTS in 1988. They show how sensitive placement rates were to the general level of demand for labour. The slump of 1980-81, when many firms collapsed, particularly in manufacturing industries, precipitated a very fast rise in unemployment. The recession was mirrored in the placement rates for TOPS/OJTS trainees, which fell by well over 20 percentage points between the first quarter of 1980 and the first quarter of 1981. Annual figures, where seasonal variations are smoothed out, reveal the same disastrous picture. The total proportion of trainees in employment three months after their course was 71 per cent in the financial year 1979/80, with 61 per cent in jobs using their skills. In 1980/81 these figures fell to 54 per cent and 44 per cent respectively; in 1981/82 to 48 per cent and 39 per cent.[1]

Thus at the time when the number of places on TOPS/OJTS first started to be cut, the results of the regular follow-up surveys were

Figure 5.1 Proportion of TOPS/OJTS trainees in employment three months after completing training; quarterly, 1980-1988

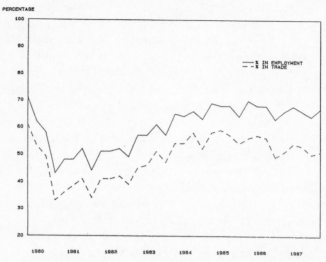

Source: Training Agency OJTS Follow-up Survey: Results for 1987/88.

producing a series of discouraging results that must have made it difficult for the programme's supporters to argue the case for maintaining funding. The emphasis of funding shifted to schemes specifically targeted on the unemployed. Yet placement rates for TOPS/OJTS courses recovered much more quickly than the general economic gloom of the first half of the eighties would lead one to expect. Unemployment nationally did not start to fall until the summer of 1986, but TOPS/OJTS placement rates were already rising again in 1982, and by 1985 were nearly back to their 1980 level. This could only have been achieved because the programme, helped by its own regular monitoring of placement rates for different types of courses, was correctly identifying the new openings in the labour market, and training men and women who were willing to move into them. Sadly, its achievements did not save it from abolition by a government that was convinced that state intervention in adult training was wrong.

Placement rates for women

As we saw in Chapter One, one consequence of the disappearance of TOPS/OJTS and the launch of Employment Training was to greatly

Figure 5.2   Proportion of TOPS/OJTS trainees in employment three months after completing training, by sex; quarterly 1979-82

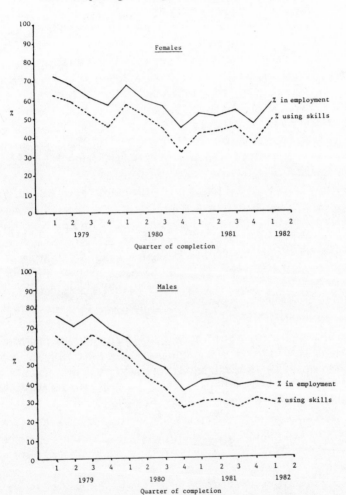

Source: Dunne, P. and Elias, P. (1986); reproduced by kind permission of the authors.

73

reduce the number of places for women on government training programmes. This consequence may have been unforeseen, but it was nonetheless real. We need therefore to ask whether the placement rates for women gave any justification for cutting public expenditure on women's training relative to expenditure on men.

The regular monitoring programme for TOPS/OJTS did not report placement rates separately for men and women. However these were calculated as part of a separate research project which re-analysed data from the follow-up surveys for the years 1979 to 1982.[2] Sex-specific placement rates for these years are given in Figure 5.2. Comparing part (b) of the figure with part (a) shows that the slump in placement rates between 1979 and 1981 was much greater for male trainees than for females, and that women's placement rates recovered more quickly than men's. Because of the nature of the industrial restructuring that was taking place at this time, demand for female labour remained more buoyant than the demand for male labour. The result was that by the first quarter of 1982 the overall employment rate for female trainees three months after completing training was a full 20 percentage points higher than the corresponding rate for men. For both sexes, the 'in trade' placement rate shadowed the overall placement rate very closely, so sex differences on this measure were very similar to those described above.

Although there are no separate figures for men and women trainees from the regular monitoring programme after 1982, from the second quarter of 1983 onwards figures are available on a consistent basis for the separate 'planning groups' or training fields into which TOPS/OJTS courses were divided. As the large majority of trainees on secretarial courses and on clerical and commercial courses were women and the large majority of trainees in the remaining planning groups were men this division between planning groups can be used as a proxy for male/female differences.[3]

Figure 5.3 plots the placement rates for this two-way classification of planning groups from 1983 up until 1988, with part (a) of the figure giving overall placement rates and part (b) giving placement rates 'in trade', in jobs relevant to the training received. In both cases placement rates for clerical/secretarial training remained superior to placement rates in the other, predominantly male training fields until the mid-eighties, when the gap between them started to close. This coming together was due initially to the recovery in the construction

Figure 5.3 Proportion of TOPS/OJTS trainees in employment three months after completing training, by course type; quarterly, 1983-1988

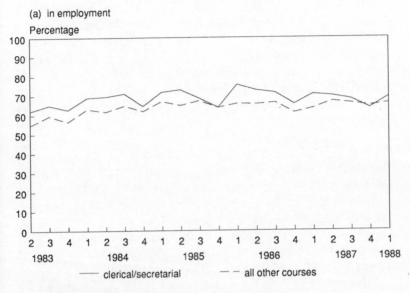

(a) in employment

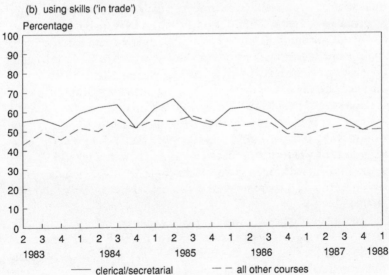

(b) using skills ('in trade')

Source: MSC/Training Agency TOPS/OJTS Follow-up Survey results for 1983-88 (own calculations).

industry, which was an important source of employment for male trainees, but as the decade progressed the economic recovery spread to other industries in which male trainees were seeking work. Nevertheless, when TOPS/OJTS was closed down in 1988, placement rates for the courses on which the majority of trainees were women remained as least as good as, if not slightly better than, placement rates on the courses done largely by men. Thus the regular monitoring of TOPS/OJTS gave no reason for supposing that money invested in training women was any less well spent than money invested in training men.

Evaluating TOPS/OJTS

The regular follow-up surveys of TOPS/OJTS were an extremely valuable source of information, but they gave only a partial picture of the effectiveness of the training programme. They kept contact with trainees only for the first three months after their course, but the importance of the concept of training for stock meant that it was crucial to find out what happened to trainees in the long-term. Thus trainees needed to be followed over a much longer period.

The regular monitoring was also incomplete in that it gave no indication of what would have happened to the trainees if they had not received any training. Trainees on TOPS/OJTS were by definition at a stage of transition in their working lives: some had lost their job, some wanted to change their job, and some wanted to start work again after a long break. It is very plausible that without training they would not have fared as well as they did. On the other hand, it could be argued that the kind of people who choose to go on training courses - and the kind of people who are selected for such courses - are already well-motivated and would be likely to do better than other people regardless of whether they received training or not. The only way to test this is to match trainees with other people in similar circumstances who have not had training, and to compare the progress of the two groups.

The Evaluation Study was far from definitive, but it substantially increased our knowledge about the value of the TOPS/OJTS model of training. In the first place, the study followed trainees up for a much longer period than the regular follow-up surveys. Trainees finished their courses during the second half of 1986 and were first interviewed in the autumn of 1987. They were contacted again by means of a postal questionnaire in the spring of 1989, more than two years after their courses had ended. Throughout this period there was a steady fall in national levels of unemployment, and so the timing of the study provided a test of whether, as the demand for labour improved, trainees who could not find work immediately or who got work in a different field from that in which they had trained were gradually able to move into suitable jobs. In the second place, the Evaluation Study incorporated a comparison sample, which allowed some conclusions to be drawn, albeit tentatively, about the difference that training made to trainees' lives. These comparisons form the subject matter of Chapter Eight.

The rest of this chapter reports the findings of the Evaluation Study on trainees' chances of finding work. It explores the longer term placement rates of trainees, how well placement rates for women compared to rates for men, and whether there were any differences between the placement rates of women who had been away from work for a long time and women who had recent work experience. Finally it asks whether there were any types of courses or personal characteristics that helped some trainees to find work more easily than others. The next chapter examines the kind of career changes that training enabled women to make, while Chapter Seven studies the effect that training had on their earnings and compares this with the effect on men's.

Long term placement rates

The Evaluation Study provided a good deal of support for the policy of training for stock. The interviews with trainees which were conducted in autumn 1987 recorded details of all jobs held since completing training the previous year. These show that 62 per cent of trainees were in work three months after finishing their course. This is very close to the estimate derived from the MSC's own regular follow-up surveys, which give a mean overall placement rate over the last quarter of 1986 and the first quarter of 1987 of 65 per cent.

The figure of 62 per cent in work three months after leaving training was however a substantial underestimate of the long-term placement rate. Ten months after the end of their course, the number of trainees in work had risen to 75 per cent, and by the time of the postal follow-up in spring 1989, more than two years after the end of training, it had grown to 83 per cent.[4] The long-term placement rates thus put the returns to the government's investment in adult training in a much more favourable light than the three month follow-up surveys, which are in many ways an unfinished story. In the longer term a third as many more trainees were in work than had found jobs after only three months.

Long-term placement rates in jobs relevant to the training received were also encouraging. Three months after the end of training the Evaluation Study showed that 48 per cent of trainees were 'in trade', again very close to the estimate of 50 per cent derived from the regular follow-up studies for the two relevant quarters. By ten months after the end of training the proportion of trainees using their skills had grown to 57 per cent, and the figure remained at this level at the last contact with trainees in spring 1989.

In 1987 employment for women was still growing more quickly than for men, and this meant that women trainees found work more

Figure 5.4   Percentage of trainees in work over the ten months after the end of their course, by sex

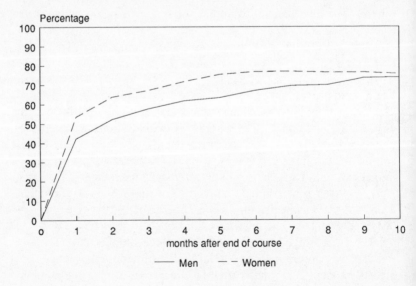

Source: Evaluation Study (base numbers: men 375, women 319).

quickly than men did.[5] Figure 5.4 plots the proportions of men and women in work in each month over the ten months after the end of their training. Three months after the end of their course, 67 per cent of women trainees were in a job, compared to only 58 per cent of men. By ten months afterwards the gap had narrowed substantially, and when the trainees were last contacted in spring 1989 the proportions were still very similar, with 82.3 per cent of women and 83.6 per cent of men in work.

Not only did women trainees find work more quickly than men, they also had a better chance of finding work that made direct use of the skills in which they had trained. In this case their advantage remained undiminished two years after they had finished their course. This was perhaps bound to be so, given that they both trained and worked in a much narrower range of occupations than men did. Nevertheless, the outcome was that the relevance of training to subsequent employment was very direct in the case of women.

In the Evaluation Study the classification of whether a trainee was 'in trade' was based on the same question that was standardly used in the MSC's own three-month follow-up surveys of trainees. For every job trainees had held after the end of their courses, they were asked how often they used the skills that they had learned on their course. As Figure 5.5 shows, 64 per cent of women trainees were using their skills 'some or all of the time' ten months after the end of their course, compared to only 51 per cent of male trainees. Though the proportion of male trainees in work grew steadily over these ten months, the proportion getting work in jobs relevant to their training did not grow at quite the same rate, and doubtless some men gave up looking for work using their skills and settled instead for any job they could find. As a result the proportion of male trainees who were using their skills declined from four-fifths of the total number in work one month after the end of the course to two-thirds ten months afterwards. In contrast over the same period the proportion of women who were in jobs which used their skills remained constant, at around four-fifths of the total number in work. By spring 1989 a substantial difference remained between the sexes, with 54 per cent of all male trainees working 'in trade', compared to 65 per cent of women.

Almost all of the trainees (men and women) who were working out of trade at the time they were interviewed in autumn 1987 said that they had tried to get a job which made greater use of what they had

Figure 5.5 Percentages of trainees in work using the skills in which they had trained over the ten months after the end of their course, by sex

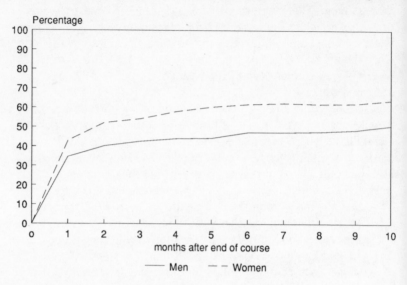

Source: Evaluation Study (base numbers: men 375, women 319).

learned on their course. Only a sixth of the group - a mere four per cent of all trainees - had been offered a job which would have used their skills and had turned it down. For the most part, working in a job which made little or no use of the training they had received was a decision that was forced on them, not a step that was taken in wanton disregard of the investment that the country had made in their training.

Placement rates for women returners

As we have seen, a significant proportion of women who trained under TOPS/OJTS had not worked for a number of years, and the needs of women returners were particularly prominent in the planning of refresher courses. Training women returners could be considered much more of a gamble than training either men or women who already had a good work record, and so placement rates for this group are of particular interest.

To examine these, we divide women trainees into four groups: women who went onto their course straight from a job, women who had worked at some time during the year preceding their course but were not in work in the month immediately before it started, women who had last worked between one and four years before the start of their course, and women who had not worked for five or more years beforehand. It would be misleading to equate these groups with women who had and had not a career break as a number of those who were in work when they started their course had a career break earlier and had since returned to work. This fact held some significance for the function that adult training served for them, as we shall discover in the next chapter. For the moment, however, we will focus on the relative placement rates for women who came into training straight from a job and women for whom training marked the end of a period away from work.

Figure 5.6 plots the proportion of women trainees in work over the ten months after the end of their course separately for each of these four groups. The numbers in the groups are small and so the plots are somewhat erratic, but one pattern is clear. Women who enrolled on their course straight from a job found work much more quickly afterwards than women who had been away from work, and they maintained their superior employment rate throughout the following ten months. Seventy-two per cent of women who came straight from a job were already in work in the first month after leaving their course, and ten months afterwards more than 90 per cent of them were in a job. These women who had very recent work experience were clearly in a strong position to compete for jobs.

However a second pattern can also be seen: for women trainees who had not been in work immediately before their course, the length of time they had been away appeared to make little difference to their subsequent chances of finding work. One month after the end of training placement rates for women who had been away from work for less than a year, women who had been away for one to four years, and women who had been away for five years or more lay within four percentage points of each other. Ten months afterwards there were still fewer than six percentage points separating these three groups.

By the time the postal survey was carried out, more than two years after the end of their course, the difference in placement rates between women who went into training straight from a job and women who

Figure 5.6 **Percentage of women trainees in work over the ten months after the end of their course, by the length of time since they had last worked before the start of their course**

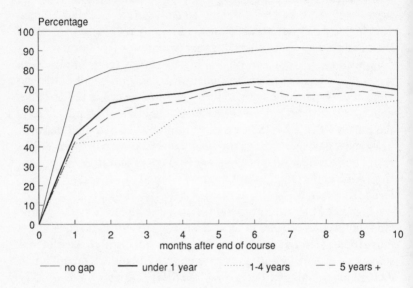

Percentage

months after end of course

— no gap ── under 1 year ⋯⋯ 1-4 years ─ ─ 5 years +

Source: Evaluation Study (base numbers: no gap 108, under 1 year 78, 1-4 years 50, 5 years or more including women who had never worked 67).

had been away from work before their course was very much reduced. At this point well over four-fifths of all women who had been away from work were in paid employment.

Differences in 'in trade' placement rates between women who went into training straight from a job and women who had been away from work for a while were similar to the differences in overall placement rates. Women who entered their course straight from a job found work using the skills in which they had trained more quickly than women who were not in work before they started training and maintained their advantage over the next ten months. Otherwise the length of time that women had been away from work did not make much difference. In spring 1989, women who had entered training straight from work were still substantially more likely to be in jobs which used their skills than women who had been away from work before their course; nevertheless the rate for the latter had increased to over 60 per cent, and was better than the corresponding figure for male trainees.

To sum up, placement rates for women returners, though not as high as placement rates for women who came into training straight from a job, were nevertheless very respectable, and in relative terms they improved over time. In addition, women who had been away from work for a very long time appeared to be just as good a risk in terms of training investment as women whose absence from work had been of only short duration.

Part-time work

Though more women than men found work relevant to their training after their course, in assessing the contribution of TOPS/OJTS to Britain's skills needs we need also to take into account the fact that women are much more likely than men to work only part-time. Against this we should set the fact that women's training courses were much more likely than men's to be part-time, and therefore carried much lower costs.

In fact, the majority of women who found work after their courses got full-time jobs. Three months after training, 64 per cent of all women trainees in jobs were working full-time, and 36 per cent were working part-time (representing 43 per cent and 24 per cent respectively of all women trainees). The second half of the 1980s was a period of rapid growth in part-time opportunities for women across the country as a whole, and though by ten months after training the proportion of women trainees in work who were working part-time had grown only marginally to 37 per cent, by spring 1989, this proportion had increased to 45 per cent. For male trainees, part-time work was of negligible importance, with only three per cent taking part-time work after leaving their course.

If we divide women into four groups according to the length of time they had been away from work before their course, as we did in Figure 5.6, we again find surprisingly little difference between those who had been away from work for a while and those who went into training straight from a job. In the first job they took after their course, full-time workers formed a clear majority over part-time workers in all four groups. Though women who had been away from work for a long time were slightly more likely to take a part-time job than women who went into training straight from a job, the difference was not great, and by spring 1989 it had narrowed still further.

Table 5.1 sets out how these different groups of women moved between full-time and part-time work. In part (a) of the table we see that, altogether, 77 per cent of women who had last worked full-time (no matter how long ago) and who got work after their course stayed in full-time work, while 23 per cent switched to part-time work. Amongst the women whose last job had been part-time and who got work afterwards, 43 per cent moved into full-time work and 57 per

Table 5.1 Women's movements between full-time and part-time work before and after training

	1st job after training		Total		Total working full-time & part-time before training
	full-time %	part-time %	%	N	%
(a) All women trainees					
last job before training:					
full-time	77	23	100	133	57
part-time	43	57	100	101	43
Total	62	38	100	234	100
(b) In work immediately before course					
last job before training:					
full-time	95	5	100	46	45
part-time	45	54	100	56	55
Total	67	33	100	102	100
(c) Away from work over 1 year before course					
last job before training:					
full-time	60	40	100	51	76
part-time	32	68	100	17	24
Total	53	47	100	68	100

Source: Evaluation Study.

cent stayed in part-time work. As more women had last worked full-time before their course than had worked part-time, the result was a small net increase in the proportion of women working full-time, from 57 per cent to 62 per cent. This might suggest a relatively poor pay-off to training in terms of increasing the extent of women's participation in the labour force, but such a conclusion ignores the fact that many of the women whose last job before their course had been full-time had been away from work for several years. If this is taken into account we get a quite different picture.

To understand this we need to look at part (b) of the table, which refers to the women who were in employment immediately before their course. Before training, 45 per cent of these women were in full-time work and 55 per cent in part-time work. Of those who were in full-time work, 95 per cent went back to full-time work after their course, whilst of those who were in part-time work, only 55 per cent stayed part-time and 45 per cent moved over into full-time work. The result was a substantial *increase* in the proportion working full-time, from 45 per cent to 67 per cent. Take next the women who had been away from work for a year or more, whose movements are shown in part (c) of the table. Seventy-six per cent of these had last worked full-time, many before they had stopped work to have children, and 40 per cent of those who had last worked full-time switched to part-time work after their course. In addition, the women who had last worked part-time were much more likely to return to part-time work after their course than to switch to full-time work. The result was a *decrease* in the proportion working full-time, from 76 per cent to 53 per cent.

Thus while, at a superficial level of analysis, participation in TOPS/OJTS did not seem to have any marked effect on the balance between part-time and full-time employment, on more detailed analysis we can detect two opposite trends, which at the aggregate level tend to cancel each other out. Women returners were indeed likely to be looking for part-time work as their first step back into the labour market, but for women who were in work immediately before their course, training was accompanied by a marked growth in full-time employment.

Women's use of their skills

Women used the skills they had acquired on their course in a variety of different ways, and many of them described these in the spontaneous comments which they added to the postal survey. Very often the relevance of their new skills to their jobs was direct and straightforward, as for this woman:

> The word processing skills have proved a great bonus as this is the newest skill I required and I use it continuously.

Even when the skills were not an integral part of the job, they could still be very helpful:

> At some point during the past year everything that was learnt on the course has been used - particularly the training on computers. Having learnt to type and use a word-processor is very useful to direct my own secretary or to use the word-processor for producing documents after office hours. Experience with computers has helped in...liaising with a computer consultant.

Sometimes skills that seemed at first to be unused were drawn on later as the job developed:

> Although initially employed as a book-keeper, I have since been asked to help with the typing. The course had given me experience with electronic typewriters which I found very useful. We also acquired a computer which we use for word-processing mostly, and the computer applications and word-processing courses have both proved very useful. As I was the only person who had any experience with computers it was left to me to learn how to use it and to train others!

In other cases, specific skills which were not used directly were nevertheless helpful in enabling the possessor to adapt to new situations:

> When I did finally manage to find employment, the office did not have a word-processor, but we have an electronic typewriter, which I found quite similar (apart from the VDU). The Co-op will soon have a computer and I feel I will soon learn to operate it because of my word-processing experience.

> The course was useful for the skills it gave me rather than the specific knowledge about electro-mechanics. As it happens, I found myself working for the building trade...but the general rules of drawing, drawing office procedures, CAD operation, etc. seem to apply for all disciplines. Also, comparing the 'reality of the drawing office' to the course I can see that the teaching was of very high quality, and

prepared us to always try for perfection, punctuality and responsibility.

This and other comments suggest that the 'in trade' placement rate is perhaps too stringent a criterion by which to judge the usefulness of training. Not only could skills be adapted to new situations, but also a number of women felt that the value of their course lay as much in the qualities of application and commitment which it demonstrated to employers as in the actual content of the training:

> I do not use a word-processor in the job I do, however I found it useful doing the course because it helped me find a job. An employer is more likely to take someone on because it shows you are willing to learn and further your knowledge in different schemes.

> When I started looking for work I felt that the fact I hadn't worked for eight years went against me, though I knew I was capable of doing the job. It was a plus in my favour that I had been on these courses. It showed that I had taken the time and trouble to keep up to date with modern office procedure.

These women argued that, although they might not be making direct use of their new skills, they could not have reached their present position without the training course:

> I think the course is very useful, especially for women going back after having a family. Even if you do not use all you learn on the course, it is a stepping-stone for getting a job.

> For someone in my position (two young children, no work experience for some years) the course was invaluable. I am certain that, but for this course, I would not have obtained my first position, and would therefore not be in my present situation.

On top of these benefits, we also need to take into account the very important gains in self-confidence that many women made that were described in Chapter Three. Without these many women would have found it very difficult to apply for jobs. Let one final comment stand for these:

> Personally while I was on the course and a few months after the course, I felt that it was a waste of time, money and effort. But the true value of this course for me personally was attitude toward doing things, things which I thought could not be done by me. I believe in myself now, and the course was the basis.

Placement rates on the Employment Training programme

As TOPS/OJTS was closed down partly in order to release funds for the Employment Training programme, there is a good deal of interest in comparing placement rates on the two schemes. Regular follow-up surveys of ET trainees began in April 1989, and since July 1989 these have been conducted on similar principles to the government's previous regular TOPS/OJTS follow-up studies, the last of which took place in the first quarter of 1988. First results were not made public until November 1990, a delay which occasioned some comment amongst critics of ET. Eventually results were published not separately for each quarter but aggregated over the period July 1989 to March 1990.[6] It was immediately obvious that ET was much less likely to lead to a job than the programme which it displaced.

During this period the proportion of men and women leaving ET who were in work three months afterwards was 38 per cent. The last ever follow-up survey for TOPS/OJTS, for the quarter ending March 1988, showed that the corresponding proportion for that scheme to be 67 per cent. These figures are set out in Table 5.2. Both may be over-estimates, though we cannot say by how much, the reason for being that neither makes any allowance for non-respondents, who according to all available evidence were less likely than trainees who returned their questionnaire to have found a job. This bias could have

Table 5.2 **Placement rates on TOPS/OJTS compared with Employment Training**

| | In work 3 months after training | | |
| | TOPS/OJTS | | ET |
	all trainees 1st quarter 1988 %	long-term unemployed 1986 %	all trainees July 89- March 90 %
all in work	67	47	38
in work in trade	51	35	23 (estimate)

Sources: Column 1: TOPS/OJTS Follow-Up Survey 1987/88.
Column 2: Evaluation Study.
Column 3: Employment Department (1990a) (including own calculations).

a significant effect on the results, as response rates were not good in either survey. Response was however better in the TOPS/OJTS follow-up survey (58 per cent) than in the ET survey (under 50 per cent), so the difference in placement rates between the two schemes may in reality have been greater than the 29 per cent gap indicated by the uncorrected figures.

At the beginning of this chapter trends were shown in placement rates for TOPS/OJTS over the 1980s, and we noted how heavily these rates depended on the state of the labour market. This fact affects the comparison between TOPS/OJTS and ET, for TOPS/OJTS was closed down a year before the first follow-up surveys for ET were conducted, and there are no figures for the two programmes that relate to the same labour market conditions. However in January 1988 when the last TOPS/OJTS follow-up survey began, seasonally adjusted unemployment in Great Britain stood at 2.6 million. By July 1989, when the first comparable ET follow-up survey started, seasonally adjusted unemployment in Great Britain had fallen to 1.7 million, and though the fall in unemployment had levelled off by the start of the new year, nevertheless unemployment during the period covered by the ET follow-up results stood at its lowest level since the start of the decade. A glance back to Figure 5.1 shows that placement rates for TOPS/OJTS reached their nadir in the fourth quarter of 1980, when British industry was experiencing many plant closures and unemployment was soaring. Yet even in those difficult years placement rates for TOPS/OJTS never fell as low as they were for ET in the relatively prosperous year of 1989.

There was, of course, a critical difference between OJTS/TOPS and ET, namely that while the large majority of entrants to ET are long-term unemployed, only 27 per cent of trainees on TOPS/OJTS fell into this category. One of the problems that unemployed people have to face is that, other things being equal, the longer they have been unemployed, the more difficult they find it to get a job. They themselves lose heart and their skills grow rusty, and employers are reluctant to hire people whom they regard as having a poor work record. On these grounds, therefore, even if the training given on ET were of equal standard to the training on TOPS/OJTS, we would expect placement rates on ET to be worse.

However, in the Evaluation Study it was possible to identify TOPS/OJTS trainees who were long-term unemployed before they started their course, and to calculate placement rates for this group separately. These rates are also given in Table 5.2. In fact 47 per cent of TOPS/OJTS trainees in 1986 who had been unemployed for six months or more before entering the scheme were in work three months after the end of their course - nine per cent more than the estimate of 38 per cent for ET trainees, and at a time when national levels of unemployment were much higher. Furthermore, 35 per cent of long-term unemployed trainees on TOPS/OJTS were in jobs which used the skills in which they had been trained, compared to an estimated 23 per cent on ET.[7] It is hard to avoid the conclusion that TOPS/OJTS was considerably more successful than ET in getting people into jobs, even if they were long-term unemployed.

This conclusion is underlined by the fact that the biggest difference between the placement rates for TOPS/OJTS and ET lay in the proportions getting full-time work. The regular follow-up surveys of TOPS/OJTS did not distinguish part-time from full-time employment, but this distinction was made in the Evaluation Study. Forty-six per cent of TOPS/OJTS trainees leaving their course in 1986 were in full-time employment three months after training, compared to 26 per cent of ET trainees in 1989/90. In addition, rather more TOPS/OJTS trainees found part-time work (eleven per cent compared to seven per cent on ET), though the proportion becoming self-employed - five per cent - was the same on both schemes. The fact that self-employment was a relatively more common outcome for ET trainees who found work than for TOPS/OJTS trainees was almost certainly a result of the big role played in ET by the construction industry, where labour-only subcontracting is very widespread.

Placement rates for different types of training

In order to fill out the picture of placement rates on TOPS/OJTS we need also to explore whether some types of courses were more helpful to trainees than others. This was a question which was of constant concern to the Manpower Services Commission in its own regular monitoring of TOPS/OJTS. As all trainees were followed up three months after they completed their course, it was possible to find out quite quickly which courses were succeeding and which were failing in getting trainees into jobs, and to modify the programme of courses accordingly. In the Evaluation Study it is possible to look at such questions only in very general terms because of the much smaller size of the sample.

Not enough women did technological or manual courses to permit sensible comparisons in the Evaluation Study with placement rates for women on clerical and secretarial courses. However, if we take men and women together, something can be said about these three different types of training. Clerical and secretarial trainees had widely applicable skills for which there was strong demand, and they were able to get jobs using those skills fairly quickly. By autumn 1987 58 per cent of clerical and secretarial trainees were 'in trade', compared to 55 per cent of technological trainees and 46 per cent of manual trainees. Technological trainees, on the other hand, whilst having skills which were in demand, were searching for work in a more specialised market. It took them longer to find work than either of the other two groups, and there was some evidence that they were more likely to have to move home to get it. Nevertheless, by the second month after leaving their course their employment rate was rising very quickly, and by ten months afterwards they had overtaken both the other two groups. In spring 1989 technological trainees still had the highest overall employment rate at 86 per cent, compared to 81 per cent and 80 per cent respectively for trainees on clerical and secretarial courses and on manual courses.

The employment rate for manual trainees also improved steadily over the ten months after the end of the course, and by ten months afterwards it had - just - overtaken the employment rate for clerical and secretarial trainees. However this improvement was achieved at the cost of a substantial number of manual trainees taking work in a field different from that in which they trained, and the proportion of all manual trainees who were using their skills fell from 87 per cent of all those in work in the first month after the course to 67 per cent ten months afterwards. Manual trainees either possessed skills which were in lower demand, or found it more difficult to move to areas of the country where their skills were in short supply, possibly because the wages they could command left them unable to meet the housing costs entailed by a move. Their problem seemed to lie in the match between the training they had done and the jobs that were on offer in the locality where they lived. Nevertheless these problems should not detract from the fact that more than half of manual trainees were in jobs relevant to their training more than two years after the end of their course.

Manual trainees were also notable for the numbers entering self-employment. The proportion who became self-employed rose from six per cent in the first month after training to 12 per cent ten months afterwards and 18 per cent in spring 1989. By this date, 22 per cent of all manual trainees in work were self-employed, and three-quarters of these worked in the construction industry. The term 'self-employment' can, however, mean many different things. In survey data it is very difficult to distinguish independent tradesmen from labour-only subcontractors who are effectively selling only their own labour 'on the lump'; indeed the borderline between these two situations is not well defined. Our sample appeared to include a majority in the latter category, though this classification was at best approximate. Despite, therefore, the numbers of manual trainees who became self-employed, not many new businesses were set up. Indeed, trainees who had it in mind to set up their own business were likely to have been directed towards the government's 'Training for Enterprise' programme instead of adult skills training.

Which trainees benefited most?
One of the main features which distinguished TOPS/OJTS from training programmes designed specifically for the unemployed was the lack of formal restrictions on entry. Nevertheless, as long as there were more people wanting training than there were places available, the question of how trainees should be selected had to be confronted, and this raised a dilemma. On the one hand it made sense to offer places to the applicants who seemed most likely to succeed, but on the other hand there was a reluctance to deny entry to men and women who may have had a higher risk of failure, but who, if they did succeed, stood to gain a great deal. This dilemma led to varying policies being adopted in different parts of the country, with some areas keeping an open door to entrants and accepting high wastage rates while other areas selected entrants more carefully. It is therefore of some interest to discover what difference the kind of factors used in the selection process, such as educational qualifications and previous work experience, made to the subsequent progress of trainees.

This kind of question is best tackled by statistical modelling, which allows us to look at the effect of any one factor, such as ethnic origin, while holding constant a whole range of other factors, such as age, sex and qualifications. In this case the appropriate technique was what is somewhat confusingly known as 'survival analysis'. Two models were fitted, the first to predict the number of months it took trainees to get a job after they left their course, the second to predict the number of months it took to get a job using the skills in which they had trained. So that the effects of different types of courses could be explored, these models used data for both men and women. The two models are given in Appendix Two (Models 1 and 2).[8]

Model 1, which analysed the time it took to get a job regardless of whether that job was using the skills or not, confirmed what Figure 5.4 had indicated, namely that when many other relevant factors were held constant, women trainees still had a significantly better chance than men of finding work quickly. It also showed that, other things being equal, the higher the unemployment rate in the local area where trainees lived (the 'travel-to-work area', as defined by the Department of Employment) the longer it took them to get work. Though this finding is hardly surprising, it should not be overlooked as it sets the context in which the importance of other factors should be assessed. Older trainees, members of ethnic minorities, and trainees with a disability or health problem also took significantly longer to get work than others.

Trainees' own work histories also had an important effect on the speed with which they found work after leaving TOPS/OJTS. Being unemployed before the start of the course reduced the chances of getting work, while the longer the total time that the trainee had worked in the years leading up to the course, the better were the chances of finding a job afterwards. Clearly employers still need to be persuaded that training unemployed people can make them into productive employees. Qualifications held before starting training proved to be unrelated to how quickly trainees got work after their course. This was probably because of the association between good qualifications and a high degree of specialisation in a technological field, and hence the need for a longer job search period. However trainees who left full-time education between the ages of 17 and 19 found work significantly more quickly than those whose education was either shorter or longer.

Turning now to the effect of variations amongst courses rather than differences between individual trainees, the finding was that none made any statistically significant difference to how long it took to get work. Once the local unemployment rate, age, sex, previous work history and other family and personal characteristics were taken into account, the differences between the placement rates of trainees on technological, clerical/secretarial and manual courses disappeared, as also did the differences between courses at technical, skilled and operative level. Thus, allowing for their differing clienteles, it seems that the various types of courses offered by TOPS/OJTS were equally helpful to trainees. This may be because TOPS/OJTS was a programme with a long history which had been continuously monitored and adapted, in the course of which unpopular and unsuccessful courses would be weeded out. The results of Model 1 could be seen as testimony to the value of this approach.

So far we have talked only about which variables significantly influenced the time it took trainees to find work, and have said nothing about the size of their effects. We can get an idea of this by introducing a hypothetical woman trainee, whom we shall call our 'baseline woman'. Let us assume she did a clerical/commercial course in a college and obtained a recognised qualification, and that she was married with two children (neither under five), aged 34, and had been a full time housewife since before 1980. Suppose also that she left school at 16 with O Level GCEs, and lived in an area with the average level of unemployment for the areas where TOPS/OJTS trainees lived. The results of Model 1 enable us to say that if our baseline woman were ten years older, her chances of entering work would be ten per cent less, and if she were only 20 years old, unmarried with no children, but with an eight month spell of unemployment before starting her course and a year's work experience since 1980, they would be 15 per cent less. If, moreover, this 20 year old were black, her chances of entering work in any given month would be one third below the chances of the baseline woman.

The second multivariate model (Model 2 in Appendix Two) was designed to predict the number of months it took trainees to get a job using the skills in which they had trained. Obviously this was highly correlated with the time taken to get a job of any kind, and the results were similar in many respects. Women's superior placement rates were still apparent after controlling for other factors. In addition the effects of the local unemployment rate and of unemployment before starting training remained statistically significant, as did health and age of leaving full time education, and differences among training courses were still insignificant. However some factors which were significant in Model 1 were not significantly associated with the time it took to get a job using the skills: these were age, membership of an ethnic minority group, and the number of months spent in employment since 1980. Furthermore, getting a recognised qualification at the end of the training course, which was insignificant in Model 1, was a significant predictor of the chances of getting a job 'in trade'. For our baseline woman, getting a recognised qualification meant that her chances of finding work were greater by 12 per cent. This is an encouraging finding, and, taken in conjunction with the insignificance of age and ethnic origin in Model 2, suggests that appropriate training leading to a recognised qualification may go some way towards reducing inequalities in the labour market.

Notes to Chapter Five

1. Unpublished Manpower Services Commission memorandum, *TOPS vocational courses: Report on 1982/83 follow-up surveys*, October 1983.
2. Dunne, P. and Elias, P. (1986).
3. See Table 3.1.
4. There was a bias in the postal follow-up survey in spring 1989 towards trainees who had found work. Seventy-three per cent of trainees who responded to the postal survey had been in work when they were interviewed in autumn 1987, compared to 65 per cent of trainees who did not respond to the postal survey. Here and throughout the book figures from the postal follow-up survey have been adjusted to correct for this and other biases.
5. Institute for Employment Research (1989a and 1989b).
6. Employment Department (1990a)
7. Estimates of placement rates derived from the Evaluation Study are less affected by response bias, which tends to inflate placement rates; hence the difference between ET and TOPS/OJTS is probably greater than these figures would sugest.
8. A fuller description of these two models are given in Payne, J. (1990), pp 48-55.

6. Training and Career Change

The evidence presented in the last chapter suggests that, in terms of the sheer number of women that TOPS/OJTS was able to get into work, the investment that the government made in training them was well worthwhile. Placement rates are undoubtedly important, but they are not the whole story. The quality of the jobs trainees get also matters. In this chapter we look at the kinds of jobs women went into after their training, and how these differed from the jobs which they had done before.

We have already seen that women entered TOPS/OJTS from a variety of different backgrounds and with many different purposes in mind. For some the main goal was to get qualifications which would enable them to escape from unemployment; for others it was to refresh or update existing skills so that they could face potential employers with confidence despite not having worked for some years. Some had become trapped in low skill work because of the difficulty of combining work and family and wanted to return to the more skilled jobs they had done earlier; others were looking for a complete change of direction. Whatever their motivation, all trainees stood at a turning point in their working lives.

The interviews with trainees in the autumn of 1987 collected details not only of jobs taken since leaving training, but of all the jobs they had held since January 1980. Some trainees had been away from work for longer than that, and these people were asked about the last job they had held, no matter how long ago it had been. Information on jobs was classified in two ways, first according to the nature of the work that was done, using the CODOT system of occupational classification[1], and second, according to the industry in which the trainee worked, using the 1980 Standard Industrial Classification. Changes in both occupation and industry following TOPS/OJTS were very marked.

Occupations before and after training

Table 6.1 shows the last job that women held before their course, their first job afterwards, and the job they were in by spring 1989. It is based on those who responded to the postal survey and were in employment at that time, and who also had worked at some time before their training (though not necessarily immediately before). This reduces the sample numbers somewhat, but has the advantage that the women who appear in the first column of the table are exactly the same women as those in the second and third columns.

Forty-six per cent of women who worked both before and after their course came from clerical and related occupations, though it could have been some years since they had last had a job. After the course the proportion in clerical and related jobs increased to 85 per cent, and in spring 1989, more than two years after leaving training, 82 per cent were doing this type of work. Conversely, before their training 15 per cent had last worked in selling occupations, usually as shop assistants or cashiers at supermarket check-outs, and 23 per cent had been employed in jobs in less skilled personal service such as catering, cleaning and care assistant type work. Both these types of occupations often have poor conditions and low pay. After training, the numbers employed in selling and personal service work fell to tiny proportions. In addition there was a reduction in the number employed in manufacturing, which for our sample mostly meant women employed in semi-skilled and repetitive jobs. Meanwhile, at the upper end of the occupational scale, the proportion of women in higher level jobs, defined to include all managerial, professional and related jobs (Major Groups I to VI in Table 6.1), fell a little in the first job taken after training compared to the last job held beforehand, but had picked up again by spring 1989.

Interesting as they are, the net changes in women's jobs that followed training tell only part of the story. For example, although the proportion of women in higher level jobs declined a little after training, this does not mean that no women were upwardly mobile into higher level jobs. To look at individual job changes we need a transition matrix, like the one given in Table 6.2. Here the row headings describe the last job before training and the column headings the first job afterwards. People on the diagonal of the matrix, indicated by the numbers that are underlined, took a job after training that fell into the same broad classification as the job they held before, while

Table 6.1   Changes in the occupations of women trainees after training

		last job before course %	first job after course %	job at postal survey spring 89 %
CODOT Major Group				
I	Managerial (general management)	0	0	0
II	Prof. & rel. supporting manag. & admin.	1	4	6
III	Prof. & rel. in education, welfare & health	4	2	3
IV	Literary, artistic & sports	2	*	1
V	Professional & related in science, engineering, technology etc	0	0	*
VI	Managerial exc. general management	2	1	*
VII	Clerical & related	46	85	82
VIII	Selling	15	1	1
IX	Security & protective service	*	0	0
X	Catering, cleaning, hairdressing & other personal service	23	2	4
XI	Farming, fishing & related	1	*	0
XII	Materials processing (exc. metal)	*	0	1
XIII	Making & repairing (exc. metal & electrical)	2	1	1
XIV	Processing, making, repairing & related (metal & electrical)	0	1	0
XV	Painting, repetitive assembling, product inspecting, packaging & related	3	2	1
XVI	Construction, mining & related	0	0	0
XVII	Transport operating, materials moving & storing & related	0	0	1
XVIII	Miscellaneous	0	0	0
Total		100	100	100
(N)		(142)	(142)	(142)

* 0.5% or less, but not zero.

Source: Evaluation Study.

Note: Based on women respondents to the postal survey who had jobs at all three stages referred to in the table.

people in the other cells of the matrix moved into a different kind of work. Comparison of the row totals and the column totals shows the net change in occupations before and after training, just like Table 6.1, but the individual cells of the table reveal how that net change came about.

Table 6.2   Transition matrix for women trainees' last job before training and their first job afterwards

	manag/ prof & rel N	clerical & rel N	less skilled service N	manu- facturing N	other N	Total N
			First job after training			
last job before training						
managerial; professional & related	<u>9</u>	16	1	1	0	27
clerical & related	5	<u>102</u>	5	0	0	112
less skilled service	1	67	<u>8</u>	8	0	84
manufacturing	1	7	0	<u>2</u>	0	10
other	1	0	0	0	<u>1</u>	2
Total N	17	192	14	11	1	235

Source: Evaluation Study

Note: Based on women trainees who had at least one job before their course and at least one job afterwards.

Table 6.2 is based on a larger number of women than Table 6.1, as it looks only at movements into the first job taken after training and includes all women trainees who had a job both before and after their course, regardless of whether they responded to the postal follow-up survey or not. In order to keep within manageable dimensions, it groups the 18 CODOT Major Groups listed in Table 6.1 into five broad classes. The cell entries are not percentages, but the actual number of women in the sample who were classed in that cell.

Women in clerical and related jobs

The first thing to look at in Table 6.2 is the number of women in the cells on the diagonal, that is, women who did the same broad kind of work after training as they did before. These are the numbers that are underlined. Altogether, 122 women - more than half of the total number of women in the table - made no change in the general kind of work that they did, but the large majority of these were women whose last job before their course had been in the clerical and related field. One hundred and two out of 112 women who had held clerical and related jobs before their course stayed in the same type of work afterwards, whereas in each of the other occupational groups only a small minority of women stayed in the same kind of work.

What, then, was the point of training for these women in clerical and related jobs who did not change the kind of work they did? Their work histories before their course make the answers clear (for there was more than one answer). About a third of these women had been out of the labour market altogether before they started their course, neither working nor seeking work - and nearly half of these had been economically inactive for more than five years. For them, the main purpose of training was to refresh their skills and enable them to return to jobs at a similar level to the jobs they had left. In our research we met many women in this position. Mrs Q., for example, had been a secretary in a travel bureau before her marriage, but with four children to look after she had not done any paid work for twenty years. She joined a refresher course designed especially for women returners, 'Because I wanted to work and that was my only opportunity to get to know modern equipment'. She found full-time work immediately afterwards as a copy typist and word processor operator, but after six months in that office was able to change this for a more interesting secretarial job involving administrative duties.

Another third of the women who stayed in clerical and related jobs had been unemployed and looking for work before their course. Miss R., from the West Midlands, was one such. Having worked for nearly two decades in the office of a large retail store, she was made redundant when the branch closed down. After that, she was able to get only temporary work, and had been without work altogether for nearly two years when she started training. She said, 'I was already doing typing at night - I couldn't get a job, so I thought I'd learn more'. Her course covered a range of office skills, and after four further months looking for work, she secured a clerical job in the civil service. Like Mrs B., she was able after a while to move on to a job which suited her better. Training was very valuable for Miss R., even though she ended up doing similar work to the work she had done before, as it demonstrated to employers her commitment to work, prevented her skills from deteriorating, and encouraged her in her job search.

The remaining third of the women who stayed in clerical and related jobs after training were in employment in this field immediately before they started their course. The main reason why they wanted to train was to upgrade their skills so that they could get a better job. The following explanations were typical of these women: 'I wanted to move from reception to secretarial work'; 'It's so much easier to get a good job if you can type, and the financial rewards are greater'; 'I needed more qualifications than I already had - I knew I could earn more if I could type'; 'I wasn't going anywhere in my job - I wanted new skills'. In a few cases women sought extra skills in order to ensure that they could get a new job when circumstances enforced a change of employer, as in the case of Miss P.. who was moving out of London, or Mrs F., who needed to look for a job after working at home for many years doing the clerical work for her husband's business.

The very broad classification of jobs used in Tables 6.1 and 6.2 is too crude to reveal the improvement in wages, conditions and responsibility which many of these women enjoyed on returning to work after their course, but the improvement was nonetheless often real. Training enabled a number of women to move out of routine clerical jobs into more skilled clerical work or jobs involving computers and word processors; it enabled others to move from the typing pool to less tedious secretarial posts. The job changes were not huge and many of them would not have registered at all on the scales which are conventionally used to measure occupational mobility (which tend not discriminate at all well between the different types of jobs that are done by women), but they were important to the women concerned. Ms G., for example, was working as an administration assistant in an NHS hospital and doing very routine work when she made up her mind to study shorthand and typing, 'to improve my chances of getting a better job'. On obtaining her certificate, she spent a month 'temping', and then got a job as a sales secretary with a manufacturing firm, where she had to work much more on her own initiative.

Only a handful of women trainees whose previous experience had been in clerical and related jobs were able to achieve a greater degree of upward occupational mobility than this and to move into professional and related jobs. All of those who did so had been in work immediately before their course, or had been away from work for only a very short time. Two were secretaries who discovered an aptitude for computing and, after the appropriate training, became computer programmers; two were women who did so well as students that they were offered jobs as instructors on courses similar to the ones they had taken; and one woman, by adding office skills to her existing skills in book-keeping, was able to secure a job as a bursar in a private school. No women, however, made the transition from clerical or secretarial work into management.

There was also a tiny handful of women who had last worked in clerical and related jobs before their course but who afterwards took less skilled service employment (defined here as selling and personal service occupations). Four of these five women had been unemployed seeking work for some time before they entered TOPS/OJTS; the last had been a full-time housewife for many years. None of the five had shorthand or typing, and all had worked in jobs at the more routine end of the clerical scale. Two had already decided to give up looking for clerical and secretarial work and took courses in quite different fields; the other three took general clerical courses. Only one of these tried and failed to get clerical work; she felt that the 12 week course had been too short to be of use. One of the remaining two women, who lived in a town with very high unemployment, was offered a job as a sales assistant soon after her course, and decided to take this opportunity without looking any further for work that made more use of the skills she had acquired; the other had held a wide range of different jobs before her course (none for more than a few months) which had been interspersed with spells of unemployment, and she resumed this pattern of employment afterwards. Thus when the detailed circumstances are examined, the downward mobility experienced by these five women does not seem to give grounds for any serious worries about the effectiveness of TOPS/OJTS.

Movements out of less skilled service jobs

A very striking feature of Table 6.2 is the large number of women who moved out of less skilled service occupations into clerical and related work. Sixty-seven of the 84 women who had last worked in these kinds of jobs found clerical and related jobs after their training course, whilst only eight remained in this type of work. Indeed, one of the most important benefits of TOPS/OJTS for women was that it offered a route out of low paid service employment into more pleasant and better rewarded work.

The majority of women who took this route were in work immediately before they started training, and those who were not had been away from work for a relatively short period of time. All did clerical or secretarial courses. A number were women who had done clerical or secretarial work at some time in the past, had left their jobs in order to have a family, and had since been forced to take less remunerative work which fitted in with the demands of small children. Mrs W. was typical:

> I was 40 and the children didn't want me at home so much. I was working in the school kitchens and I knew I could do a better job than that. I thought I'd go back to my old trade.

However it was also not uncommon for women to take a clerical/secretarial course and get a job using their new skills without ever having done this type of work before. Mrs L. was 25, and despite her two O Levels and four CSEs had only ever worked as a canteen assistant. She took a word processing course - 'I wanted to get into word processing work for the good employment and pay prospects' - which in the relatively buoyant job market of London where she lived enabled her to get a secretarial job. Mrs K. had tried a variety of jobs, from machine operator to student nurse to general work in a garden centre. She did very well on her secretarial course, gaining RSA Stage 2 qualifications in typing, audio-typing and word processing, as well as English Language O Level. On completion, she found work immediately as a medical secretary in a group practice.

Under the Employment Training programme, Mrs K. and many of the other women who were in work immediately before their course started would be unable to get a training place. She was not long-term unemployed and could not be classed as a 'returner', having worked all her adult life. The only option now for women like Mrs K.who want training but cannot afford to pay for their own fees or subsistence is to take out one of the Career Development Loans that were described in Chapter One.

Women in manufacturing

Jobs in manufacturing formed another group of occupations to which very few women returned after going on TOPS/OJTS: only two out of the ten women who had last worked in factories went back to factory work afterwards. The majority of those who left factory work went into clerical and related work, and their circumstances and experiences were not dissimilar from those of women who moved from less skilled service jobs into clerical and related work. Most were women who had done office work before they had their children, and had since been forced to take factory work as they could not get any other job where the hours and travelling distances fitted in with their family commitments - like, for example, Mrs B. When her daughter reached school age, she took a job as a barmaid, but stayed only a short time because she found working at nights too exhausting. A year or so later she took another part-time job as a packer in a firm making car parts, but was made redundant after only a few months. At this point she decided to take a training course in secretarial skills, because, as she said, 'I was fed up with the jobs I was doing and wanted to get back into the office environment'. She gained Pitman's qualifications in typing and found a full-time job as a copy typist immediately afterwards.

Occasionally women who had never worked in an office before were able to make use of the opportunity provided by TOPS/OJTS to break out of factory work, though such women were unusual. Mrs U., who lived in Lancashire, had several CSEs, but since leaving school had done only semi-skilled assembly work. She passed the aptitude test for admission to a secretarial course, which she took 'to better myself - gain qualifications and do a more interesting job'. She gained basic qualifications in typing and word processing, and was able subsequently to get a series of temporary jobs as a copy typist, first with the education authority and later with a building society.

The women who left jobs in manufacturing were replaced by a similar number of women who had previously worked in less skilled service jobs, so that the total number of women employed in manufacturing was almost the same after training as it was before.

Such movements are revealed in a transition matrix like Table 6.2, though totally obscured in Table 6.1.

Most of the women who moved into manufacturing from less skilled service jobs took manual courses and got jobs using their skills, often substantially increasing their earnings in the process. Indeed, whilst most of the women who had left manufacturing had been doing repetitive semi-skilled or unskilled work as assemblers or packers, the women who went into manufacturing after training took jobs requiring a higher level of skill. However three of the women going into manufacturing did clerical/secretarial courses, and at first sight appeared to be wasting their training. The particular circumstances of each, however, showed this not to be so. One got a job as a typesetter, and was using her keyboarding and word processing skills continuously; the second was in her factory job for only a month and left it when she was offered a job as a legal secretary; whilst the third very sadly had an accident after finishing her training which left her unable to walk, though she was able to hold down a light assembly job.

Higher level jobs

Though the transition matrix showed that a small number of women trainees moved into professional and related jobs supporting management and administration, the upward mobility they experienced was off-set by a rather larger number who were downwardly mobile from higher level jobs. Of 27 women who were in higher level jobs before their course, only nine stayed in work of the same level afterwards. The large majority of these women did clerical/secretarial courses. Their experience conflicts with the rest of the evidence presented in this chapter, which indicates that training on TOPS/OJTS generally enhanced women's careers. We need therefore to look in some detail at the role that training played in their change of career. We will find that, despite the unpromising appearances, when the particular circumstances of each case are examined, the real help that training often gave to these women becomes evident.

One relatively common situation for these downwardly mobile women was that they had been working abroad, and when they settled in this country they found that their qualifications were not recognised or that the type of work they had done abroad was not available here. This was true of a third of the women who were downwardly mobile from higher level jobs, and their migration often followed their husband's employment. They included women from both Third World and European countries - a maths teacher from India, a primary school teacher from the Philippines, a night-school teacher of English in Germany, and others. Training gave women like this the chance to acquire skills that they could use in this country, even if it did mean setting their sights somewhat lower than before. For example, Mrs T. had studied for a degree in psychology in the Philippines and had worked in academic research, but needed British secretarial qualifications in order to get work in England, and Miss K., who had been a statistician in an Arab country, found that the only posts for which British employers would consider her asked for typing and word processing skills.

Another not infrequent reason why women left a higher level job was that they were disillusioned with their profession. Among the downwardly mobile women in our sample were three schoolteachers in British schools and a trained nurse; they sought secretarial work as an exit route. Mrs W. 'wanted something completely different from teaching'; Mrs S. said her reason for seeking retraining was that, 'Really, I was unhappy in the job I was doing, so I thought it was worth being trained for something else'. Some of these women turned out to be disappointed with their change of career, but they at least had the opportunity to try out an alternative.

A third group of downwardly mobile women had been forced to abandon their earlier career through a variety of unfortunate circumstances, including redundancy, ill-health, and the personal upheavals of divorce. Training gave these women the opportunity to salvage something out of the wreckage. For example, a former dental nurse said that 'after several mishaps concerning employment and illness I lost confidence in myself'; for her, the main function of training was 'to give yourself confidence'.

Finally, quite a number of the women who left higher level occupations had been doing jobs which, although requiring responsibility and skill, were nevertheless insecure or not particularly well paid. Examples included acting, night school teaching, and managing a shop. Whatever conventional gradings of occupations might indicate, these women saw their move into secure full-time secretarial jobs as a step upwards. This view was exemplified by a mother of two who had been teaching cookery in evening classes. She applied for a course 'because I wanted to go back to work full-time and I was a bit uncertain of the skills I had to offer', and one of the main benefits she felt she gained from it was 'building confidence to compete in the job market'. A similarly positive attitude was taken by women who had not worked for so many years that they believed they had no realistic chance of returning to work of equal standing to the work they had left. Mrs L., for instance, who had been the manageress of a shop in the 1970's, considered herself 'lucky to get started' in electronic assembly, while Mrs A., who had been an executive officer in a local authority nearly twenty years before, wrote, 'The scheme gave me confidence to undertake office jobs not previously undertaken, eg use a Telex machine'.

Movements between industries

As well as changing their occupation, women also often moved to work in a different industry after training. It is, of course, perfectly possible to do exactly the same kind of work within quite different industries; for example a canteen assistant in a car factory is classed as working in the engineering industry while a canteen assistant in a hospital is classed in the public service sector. Nevertheless certain types of job predominate in certain industries, and some industries tend to offer better pay and conditions of employment than others. The changes in the industries in which women trainees worked after their courses often reflected the general upgrading of their work, but they were also shaped by the opening up of opportunities in expanding sectors of the economy.

Table 6.3 reports the net changes in trainees' industry of employment that took place between their last job before their course, their first job afterwards, and their job in spring 1989, more than two years after leaving training. Like Table 6.1, it is based only on women who responded to the postal follow-up survey and had a job at that time, as well as having worked at some time before their course. The biggest change that the table shows is the sharp fall in the number of women employed in SIC Division 6. This division covers repairs as well as the distribution industry, and hotels and catering, but the majority of women in it are employed in distribution and in hotels and catering. There was a big movement out of this division in our sample despite the fact that in the country as a whole employment in this division is growing, and women's share of employment in these

Table 6.3 Changes in the industries in which women trainees were employed after training.

	last job before course %	first job after course %	job at postal survey spring 89 %
1980 SIC Division			
0 Agriculture, forestry & fishing	0	0	0
1 Energy & water supply	1	1	0
2 Extraction of minerals & ores other than fuels; manufacture of metals, mineral products & chemicals	1	3	1
3 Metal goods, engineering & vehicles	4	11	6
4 Other manufacturing	8	6	7
5 Construction	1	3	4
6 Distribution, hotels & catering; repairs	33	8	10
7 Transport & communication	3	3	3
8 Financial & business services	12	26	24
9 Other services	37	40	45
Total	100	100	100
(Base N)	(142)	(142)	(142)

* 0.5% or less, but not zero.

Source: Evaluation Study

Note: Based on women respondents to the postal survey who had jobs at all three stages referred to in the table.

industries is also increasing.[2] They are of course industries in which many jobs are low skilled, low paid and part-time.

The corresponding transition matrix is found in Table 6.4. Less than a third of the women here occupy the cells on the diagonal, that is, less than a third found work in the same broad grouping of industries as they had last worked in before their course, and overall the pattern of movements is quite complex. The most striking feature is the large number of women trainees leaving SIC Division 6 (distribution, hotels and catering, and repairs) in order to enter financial and business services, other services, and manufacturing. The extent of the fluidity between industries is shown by the fact that none of the industrial groupings in the table retained even half of the women whom they had previously employed. It is however notable that the industry which kept the largest proportion of its employees following training was in fact the biggest growth sector in the British economy during the eighties, namely financial and business services.

Table 6.4   Transition matrix for the industry of the last job before training and the first job afterwards: women

| | Industry of first job after training | | | | | | |
	0-2 N	3,4 N	5,7 N	6 N	8 N	9 N	Total N
Industry of last job before training:							
0-2: Primary industries & utilities	1		2		1		4
3,4: Manufacturing	1	5	2	1	8	8	25
5,7: Construction & Transport		1	1	2	3	4	11
6: Distribution, hotels & catering, repairs		14	5	17	18	26	80
8: Financial & business services	1	5	1	3	18	10	38
9: Other services	5	10	3	6	20	30	74
Total N	8	35	14	29	68	78	232

Source: Evaluation Study

Note: Based on women trainees who had at least one job before their course and at least one job afterwards.

Notes to Chapter Six

1. Manpower Services Commission (1972), with subsequent Supplements.
2. Institute for Employment Research (1989a).

7. Earnings

The main reason why most women work is the same as it is for men - to earn a living. Whatever the gains from vocational training in terms of enhancing personal development and opening up more interesting careers, not many women would spend time and energy in this way if at the end of it all they found themselves with lower wages than they had before. In policy terms also the effect of training on earnings is critical, as in market economies earnings are the most important measure we have of the value of a worker's labour to the economy. In studies that try to establish the 'rate of return' to investment in education and training, the increase in the earnings that a worker can command almost invariably figures as the main element in the assessment of benefits. Though earnings may be unsatisfactory and incomplete as an indicator of the gains to society that stem from public investment in a training programme, as a measure of the returns to the investment they remain highly influential.

In the case of women on TOPS/OJTS, the career changes that followed their training courses were bound to affect the level of their earnings. This chapter describes the change in the earnings of women trainees before and after training and how this compared with men, and goes on to show who amongst the women gained most in financial terms from their course.

Measuring the change in earnings

The Evaluation Study collected information about trainees' earnings before tax in their current job, if they were in work at the time of interview in autumn 1987 (on average 10 months after the end of their course), and about their earnings in their last job if they were not in work at interview but had held a job since leaving their course. In addition trainees were asked about their earnings in their last job before they started their course, though not if this job ended before January 1980. This information was used to calculate gross hourly earnings (including overtime, bonus, commission and tips, etc.) before and after training. These were then uprated to October 1987 values using the seasonally adjusted Average Earnings Index for all employees for the industrial sector in which the job was classed.[1] Finally, the difference between the uprated gross hourly earnings before and after training was computed: this was the measure of the change in earnings that was used in the analyses in this chapter.

Obviously people who had held no job before entering training and people who at the time of interview had not yet found a job after their course could not be included in these calculations. Certain other trainees were also excluded for technical reasons.[2] Together these exclusions left 371 men and women with earnings data suitable for analysis, somewhat under half of the original sample.[3] This subsample included slightly more men, more under-25's, and more trainees on technological courses than the sample as a whole. It also left out a number who could not remember what they had earned before their course and all those who prior to their course had not worked since before 1980. Such losses are, unfortunately, inevitable in a study which relies on data collected retrospectively. There is also an unavoidable degree of error in information which relies on memory, which may make the pattern of change less easy to detect, but we have no reason for supposing that there is any systematic bias.

The pattern of change

Overall, women enjoyed a modest increase in the average level of their hourly pay after their training. As Table 7.1 shows, in their last job before their course the mean earnings of women for whom we have data both before and after training were £2.99 per hour; afterwards (after taking out the increase due to inflation) they rose to £3.10 per hour. This was in contrast to the picture for male trainees, who had substantially higher earnings than women before training - £4.05 per hour - but whose earnings fell by an average of 27 pence to £3.78 after their course.

Mean gains and losses, however, give a very incomplete picture of the changes that took place. Table 7.1 also reports the standard deviations, which give a measure of the amount of variation in earnings that there was among trainees. These show that there was much less variability in the earnings of individual women trainees, both before and after training, than there was for men. This is just

111

Table 7.1   Mean earnings (uprated to October 1987 values) before and after training, by sex

| | | gross hourly earnings | | | | | |
| | | before training | | after training | | difference | |
	N	mean	s.d.	mean	s.d.	mean	s.d.
Men	200	£4.05	2.05	£3.78	1.35	-£0.27	2.10
Women	171	£2.99	1.42	£3.10	.88	+£0.11	1.39
Total	371	£3.56	1.86	£3.46	1.20	-£0.10	1.81

Source: Evaluation Study.

what the clustering of women in a much narrower range of occupations than men would lead us to expect. However the standard deviations reveal another marked pattern: for both women and men, the variation in earnings was much less after training than it was before. In effect, the earnings of women trainees were much closer to each other after training than they were before, and the same was true for men.

Figure 7.1 depicts this pattern graphically. It shows how much more bunched together were the earnings of women trainees compared to the earnings of men, which were much more evenly spread out across a wider range of earnings bands, both before and after training. However it also shows that the effect of training was similar for both sexes. Before training the earnings distributions had long tails at both ends - a number of trainees had very low earnings and still more had very high earnings. After training these tails shrank, and the distributions became much more compressed.

An alternative measure of 'average' earnings is the mode, which is the earnings band into which more people fall than any other. For men the mode before training was £3.00-£3.50, and, despite the fall of 27 pence in mean earnings, it remained unchanged afterwards; it was the loss of a few very high wages which caused men's mean earnings to drop. For women, training had a more positive effect. Although the upper tail of high wages also shrank away, there was an overall increase in pay levels. Before training, the modal earnings band for women was £2.00-£2.50; after training it rose to £2.50-£3.00 - hence the modest improvement in mean earnings for women trainees.

Figure 7.1 **Distribution of gross hourly earnings before and after training, by sex**

(50p bands)

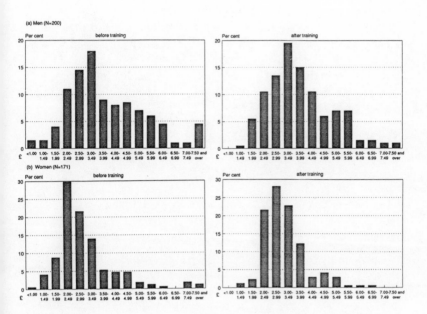

Source: Evaluation Study.

113

Table 7.2 shows what these changes meant in terms of earnings gains and losses for individual men and women. Fifty per cent of male trainees made losses and 46 per cent made gains; only 37 per cent of women trainees made losses and 58 per cent made gains. For most women, the gains or losses were fairly small: nearly half had hourly earnings after training which were within plus or minus 50 pence of their earnings before training, and two-thirds had earnings within £1.00 of the earlier figure. Nevertheless changes which were relatively modest in absolute terms were very important in relative terms when initial earnings were so low: an increase of 50 pence per hour on earnings of £2.50 per hour represents a rise of 20 per cent. Men's gains and losses were bigger than women's in absolute terms:

Table 7.2   Distribution of earnings gains and losses, by sex

	men %	women %	All %
Earnings losses	50	37	44
of which:			
-£4.00 or more	4	2	3
-£3.00 to -£3.99	4	1	3
-£2.00 to -£2.99	6	2	4
-£1.00 to -£1.99	12	8	10
-£0.50 to -£0.99	11	6	9
-£0.05 to -£0.49	12	18	15
No change (+£0.04 to -£0.04)	4	5	4
Earnings gains	46	58	52
of which:			
+£0.05 to +£0.49	13	25	18
+£0.50 to +£0.99	9	13	11
+£1.00 to +£1.99	16	16	16
+£2.00 to +£2.99	6	4	5
+£3.00 to +£3.99	*	1	1
+£4.00 or more	2	0	1
Total	100	100	100
(N)	(200)	(171)	(371)

* 0.5% or less, but not zero.

Source: Evaluation Study.

less than half involved changes of under £1.00 and going on for a quarter were changes of plus or minus £2.00 or more.

Losers and gainers
Though most of the changes in women's earnings after training were on the small side, there were some women whose hourly earnings changed substantially. For both sexes the biggest losses in earnings were experienced by those who earned most before their course, and the biggest gains were made by those who had earned least. The strength of the relationship is demonstrated in Table 7.3, which shows, for example, that people who were earning between £1.50 and £2.00 per hour before training made mean gains of 80 pence, while people earning between £4.50 and £5.00 made mean losses of 82 pence. To some extent this relationship derives from regression towards the mean, a purely artificial statistical effect which arises from random errors in our measurement of earnings. However the link between the size of gains and losses and the level of previous earnings also reflects real changes in trainee's circumstances, which can be understood in the light of their previous histories and the motivations with which they entered training.

Table 7.3   Mean difference in earnings before and after training, by level of earnings before training

hourly earnings before training	N	difference in earnings after training
£1.50 or less	14	+£1.55
£1.51 - £2.00	23	+£0.80
£2.01 - £2.50	73	+£0.75
£2.51 - £3.00	66	+£0.64
£3.01 - £3.50	60	+£0.07
£3.51 - £4.00	27	+£0.15
£4.01 - £4.50	24	-£0.34
£4.51 - £5.00	25	-£0.82
£5.01 or more	59	-£2.59

Source: Evaluation Study.

In the case of men with previously high earnings, one factor that was often involved was redundancy, frequently followed by a lengthy spell of unemployment. For such men, and especially for the older ones amongst them, retraining offered the best chance they had of re-employment, and if the level of remuneration in their new job was not as good as before, it was at least much better than the dole. Redundancy also figured occasionally in the past lives of the women trainees who after training found themselves earning considerably less than before. Mrs V., for example, had been made redundant at the age of 40 from a well paid administrative job, when the company that employed her folded. By acquiring Pitman's qualifications in audio-typing and word processing she was able to find re-employment as a secretary, and she regarded her course as 'very useful' despite the fall in income. In other cases, redundancy had been followed by work which, though well paid, was insecure or temporary. Mrs R., a widow, had stayed for over 25 years with the same firm and although she had no formal qualifications she had worked her way up to be head of accounts. When she was made redundant in 1985 she managed to get work as a financial consultant, but although the pay appeared attractive, it depended largely on commission, a situation which she found unsatisfactory. She decided to retrain, 'Because I thought you can always get a job as a secretary, whereas if you say you are an accountant they want qualifications at my age rather than experience'. Her new job as an administrative assistant with a learned society brought in much lower earnings, but at least she knew from one week to the next how much she would be taking home. Mrs T., a former restaurant manageress, had been unemployed for a year and a half after the restaurant closed down before finding a temporary job as a programme officer for a national campaign. The work was interesting and well paid, but it came to an end after three months. She was pleased when her course in new office technology led to a permanent full-time job as a medical secretary, although it meant a drop of over a pound in her hourly earnings. Thus the thickness of the pay packet was not the only consideration that was important where earnings were concerned: security and stability also mattered.

As we saw in the last chapter, other women who had previously been high earners sought training because they were dissatisfied with their job and wanted to make a change, or because some obstacle prevented them from continuing in their previous profession. Training gave such people the chance to change direction, but at the start of a new career they accepted that their earnings would be lower than in the job they had left. Miss D.'s case illustrates this. She had held an administrative position of some responsibility in London, where she had been with the same organisation for many years and had commanded a good salary. However she had been very keen to move out of London, and realised that to get a job in 'the provinces', 'At my age I needed to learn how to type and do shorthand'. She succeeded in her ambition, though it entailed a substantial reduction in her income.

There were of course a few women who failed to improve their earnings after their course not because they were deliberately embarking on a change of career, but simply because they were unable to find a job in the field in which they trained. These women very often returned to the same kind of work that they had been doing before their course, and any reduction in earnings was generally only small.

Thus although a number of women earned less after their course than they did before, virtually the same proportion judged that their course had been useful to them as in the case of women whose earnings had improved. In the postal survey, more than two years after they had left TOPS/OJTS, 67 per cent of women who were earning less than before rated their training as 'very useful' to their career in the long term compared to 69 per cent of women whose earnings were higher, and ten per cent of the losers said it was 'not useful at all' compared to eight per cent of the gainers.

Losers were, however, outnumbered by gainers. The biggest contribution to the overall gains that were achieved by women trainees came from women who managed to move out of lower level service occupations. Mrs L. was typical: a divorcee and lone parent working part-time as a kitchen assistant in a public house, she took a short refresher course which enabled her to return to secretarial work and to increase her earnings by over £1.25 per hour. Her experience was repeated many times by women in the Evaluation Study. Not only did many women improve their earnings in this way, but many of the gains they made were substantial. Earnings for women who moved from low skill service jobs to clerical and related jobs averaged £2.56 per hour before training and £3.02 afterwards - a mean gain of 46 pence. In contrast, the earnings of the small number of women who went back into the same kind of low skill service jobs after their course as they had done before changed very little - for them the average was £2.38 per hour before training and £2.45 afterwards, a gain of only seven pence. However the biggest gains of all were enjoyed by the small number of women who moved out of low skill service occupations into skilled manual occupations: though we have complete earnings data for only five such women, on average they were better off by £1.38 per hour.

Improvements in earnings were also made by women who had previously been in manual jobs in industry, which, as we saw in Chapter Two, usually meant low skilled jobs as machine operatives or packers. Useful gains were made by women who moved from jobs like this into clerical and related jobs (a mean gain of 47 pence), but even greater gains were made by the very few women who stayed in manufacturing industry but switched after training to skilled manual jobs.

Improved earnings were not confined to upwardly mobile women: there were several instances where women already employed in clerical and secretarial work were able to secure better paid jobs within the same broad class by adding extra skills to their existing repertoire. Miss B., for instance, a single woman in her early twenties, had been 'temping' for an agency doing general clerical duties. She decided to train because, 'I needed secretarial skills such as shorthand and typing', and after a three month course on which she gained the relevant Pitman's certificates, she immediately obtained a job which called for a much fuller range of skills. The change brought with it a substantial improvement in pay. Mrs L. was older, and though she was an experienced typist, she was hampered by her lack of familiarity with modern office technology. A friend told her about TOPS/OJTS and she applied for a short intensive course in the use of microcomputers. This led her into a job as a VDU operator and 66 pence per hour more than she had been earning previously. On average, however, the earnings of women who returned to clerical and related jobs after training fell by eight pence, because the gains made by women like Miss B. and Mrs L. who had been in work immediately before their course were offset by the losses of women who were returning to clerical and related work after a long break and who earned on average less in real terms on first re-entering the labour market than they had earned before.

Characteristics associated with gains and losses

As we have seen, the main route by which women bettered their earnings after the end of their course was by moving out of low skilled work in either service or manual occupations and into skilled work in either white collar or manual occupations. This was reflected in the pattern of earnings changes for women entering training from different kinds of jobs. As the first part of Table 7.4 shows, the mean earnings of women who had been in low skill service or manual work increased by 54 pence per hour after training, while the earnings of women who had been in clerical and related jobs showed little change and the

Table 7.4 Earnings before and after training for different groups of women trainees

	N	mean gross hourly earnings		
		before training	after training	difference
(a) Previous occupation				
managerial/professional & rel.	25	£4.00	£3.38	-£0.62
clerical & related	74	£3.16	£3.10	-£0.06
low skill service or manual	72	£2.47	£3.01	+£0.54
(b) Qualifications				
5 O Levels & above	54	£3.63	£3.31	-£0.32
1-4 O Levels	53	£2.68	£2.97	+£0.29
below O Level	64	£2.70	£3.03	+£0.33
(c) History				
in work in month before course	83	£2.89	£3.17	+£0.28
away from work for 1-11 months before	56	£2.99	£2.96	-£0.03
away from work for 12+ months before	32	£3.26	£3.18	-£0.08
(d) Age				
under 35	73	£2.76	£3.27	+£0.51
35 & over	98	£3.16	£2.97	-£0.19
All women	171	£2.99	£3.10	+£0.11

Source: Evaluation Study.

earnings of women who had last worked in higher level non-manual jobs dropped on average by 62 pence.

Not surprisingly, women who came from low skill service and manual work were less well qualified than others - only 18 per cent had educational qualifications equivalent to five O Level GCEs or better compared to 41 per cent of women who came from other kinds of work. They were also rather more likely to have been in work in the month before they started their course (62 per cent compared to 38 per cent of other women). In consequence, as parts (b) and (c) of the table show, women with these characteristics were much more likely to see their earnings improve than were others. This did not necessarily mean that they ended up with better earnings than women whose earnings had not increased - sometimes there was simply just too much ground to be made up. Women with no qualifications or qualifications below the standard of O Level GCE improved their earnings by an average of 33 pence per hour, whilst women who possessed the equivalent of five or more O Levels or better saw their earnings fall on average by 32 pence. Although these changes substantially narrowed the earnings gap between the two groups, they were not big enough to wipe out the advantage that the better qualified women still enjoyed: after training women with good educational qualifications earned an average of £3.31 per hour, while women with few or none earned £3.03. Similarly, training nearly eliminated the gap between women who were in work immediately before the start of their course, whose earnings went up on average by 28 pence per hour, and their colleagues, who experienced a marginal drop compared to their earnings in their last job before their course.

There was also an association between the age of trainees and the probability of gaining or losing in earnings. The last part of Table 7.4 shows that women under the age of 35 made an average gain of 51 pence per hour, compared to an average loss of 19 pence for women trainees over 35. In this case the changes meant that the earnings of younger women overtook those of older women, with average earnings of £3.27 after training compared to the £2.97 commanded by their seniors. As in the case of qualifications, the explanation for this relationship also lies in patterns of occupational mobility. Women who were downwardly mobile from either higher level non-manual or clerical and related jobs were on average older than women who stayed in these types of jobs after training, and women who moved from low skill service jobs to either clerical and related work or skilled manual work were on average younger than those who did not alter the type of work they did.

Modelling changes

In all, there was a range of factors that affected changes in earnings after training. Several of these were associated with each other and several were also related to the level of earnings before training, which itself had a very strong inverse correlation with gains and losses. To help disentangle these and get an idea of the separate importance of each factor independently of the others we need to use statistical modelling. Thus a regression model was fitted to the predict the difference in women's gross hourly earnings before and after training, which, for readers who are interested in the details, can be found as Model 3 in Appendix Two.

It must be remembered that, for obvious reasons, the women for whom we have data on changes in earnings had all succeeded sooner or later in getting a job after the end of their course. There were some factors that were found in Chapter Five to be significant predictors of the chances of getting work that did not affect the likelihood of earning more or less than before, given that a job had already been secured. Conversely, other factors that had been unrelated to the chances of getting work did turn out to have a bearing on earnings.

Before describing the results of Model 3, a slight complexity needs to be explained. The change in earnings after training could be positive or negative, as there were both gains and losses. Thus factors that were positively associated with the change in earnings led to bigger gains and smaller losses, whilst factors that were negatively associated reduced gains and increased losses. It would be would be tedious to spell this out each time, and so the reader is asked to accept that when a factor is said to 'increase gains', it should be understood to mean that it also reduced losses, and vice versa.

Let us turn, then, to the results of the model. As expected, the level of earnings before training proved to be a very significant predictor of gains. Holding all the other variables in the model constant, for every extra new penny that a woman earned before she started her course, the gains that she might expect to make afterwards were reduced by .58 of a penny. Once prior earnings were included in the model, none of the other variables which, when considered in isolation in Table 7.4, had been associated with earnings change, retained any predictive power: previous occupation, age, qualifications, and how long women had been away from work before starting training all had statistically insignificant coefficients in the multivariate analysis.

There were, however, other variables which remained significantly associated with earnings gains and losses even when the level of previous earnings was held constant. One of these was the level of unemployment in the local labour market at the time that trainees finished their course. This reduced predicted earnings gains by over three pence for each one per cent rise in the local unemployment rate. It seems likely that a high level of unemployment locally meant fewer opportunities open to women to move out of low skill, low paid jobs into better paid employment in expanding sectors of the economy.

Only a very few women in the Evaluation Study did technological courses, but the effect that doing this type of course had on their earnings was big enough to be statistically significant. Other things being equal, these women increased their earnings by 73 pence more than clerical/secretarial trainees. There was however no significant difference between the gains made by trainees on manual courses and by trainees on clerical/secretarial courses.

Women who had trained to do a completely different type of work from the work they had done before might well expect to earn less at the start of their new career than women who were building on an existing base of skills and experience. This came out quite strongly in the model: when other factors were held constant, earnings gains for women who were training in a new field were estimated to be 78 pence per hour less than for women whose course was designed to improve or update their skills, a result which was comfortably within the margins of statistical significance.

Although it can be argued that training might have indirect benefits even for trainees who do not find work using their new skills, if training is effective we ought to expect trainees working 'in trade', that is using their skills, to receive the biggest rewards from their course. This variable is therefore of particular interest in analysing the effect of training on women's earnings. The expectation was confirmed: women who found work using their skills gained, other things being equal, an estimated £1.16 pence per hour more than women who were not 'in trade'. This is a very pertinent measure of the value placed by the market on the skills these women acquired in training.

There is an interesting result concerning the effect of belonging to an ethnic minority group. It will be recalled that this factor reduced the chances of finding work of any kind after training, though not the probability of finding work 'in trade'. According to Model 3, women who were members of ethnic minorities and who succeeded in getting work had predicted earnings gains 38 pence per hour greater than non-minority trainees, a statistically significant result. This may suggest some selectivity on the part of ethnic minority trainees as to the jobs they were willing to take. It accords with the point made in Chapter Four, that women who were born abroad often had obtained quite high level qualifications in their country of birth, but these were not recognised in this country. Such qualifications would presumably make them less willing to accept low level and inappropriate employment and the consequent wastage of their new skills.

In Britain, where there is very little public provision of child care, one of the biggest factors that influences a woman's decision to work is the age of her children. In particular, having a child under school age reduces women's activity rates very markedly.[4] In the Evaluation Study there was a very strong association, once other factors had been held constant, between having a child under the age of five before starting the course and reduced earnings gains. The relationship was however more complex than this. At the bivariate level, without controlling for any other factors that might be involved, it went in the opposite direction: the gains of women with children under five were 36 pence greater than the gains of other women, despite the fact that the two groups had similar mean earnings before training. The explanation lies in a statistically significant interaction between having a child under five and the level of previous pay in their effects on earnings change. This meant that having a child under five was a disadvantage for women who before training had received very low levels of pay, but no disadvantage for women who had been better paid. Though it is easy to think of reasons why this might be so, it would be unwise to set too much store on the result. There were only a few women in the sample with children as young as this, and the result could be heavily influenced by a very small number with especially high gains or losses.

The effects of two of the other factors were also not uniform for all levels of pay before training. Firstly, there was some evidence from interaction terms fitted in the model that the extra earnings gains that came from doing a course which built on existing skills rather than one which represented a change of direction were even greater if trainees had previously earned very little. A number of the case studies we have already looked at suggest why this is so: many of the women who were in low skill jobs before they took training had family commitments which had forced them to abandon better paid jobs which they had held before their children were born. Refresher courses which renewed and upgraded their former skills very often enabled them to return to skilled white collar employment and to make substantial gains in earnings.

The second variable whose effect varied with the level of pay before training was whether the trainee found a job using the skills in which she had trained. In this case also, being employed 'in trade' benefited women whose pay had been low before training more than it benefited those whose pay had been high. The explanation is probably also connected with patterns of occupational mobility. Women who came from low skill jobs reaped the benefit of their training when they moved into the clerical and secretarial jobs that it fitted them for; if they failed to get work of this nature then they had only low paid jobs to fall back on. As Chapter Two showed, women who came from more highly paid jobs as managers, professionals and associate professionals sought training for a wider variety of reasons, often connected with their own particular personal circumstances. For them, finding work using their new skills could mean accepting lower earnings than they had before, but this was a trade-off which they were often prepared to make.

Notes to Chapter Seven

1. *Employment Gazette* Statistical Supplement 44, Jan. 1989, Table 5.1
2. Also excluded were those who refused to give any information on earnings, those who gave confused or incomplete information, and those who could not remember what their earnings had been before training. An attempt was made to collect data on earnings from self-employment, but such data are notoriously unreliable, and after consideration a decision was made also to exclude people

who were self-employed either before or after training. A few people had last worked abroad before training, and these too were omitted as we did not have the sterling equivalent of their pay. All trainees were at least 19 years of age when they started training, but a few had been younger than 18 at the time they left the last job which they had held before training. In their case the transition from youth to adult rates of pay confused the picture, and so they also were dropped from the analysis.

3. Because the original sample was so much reduced in size, all the analyses in this chapter are based on unweighted data (see Appendix Two).

4. Joshi, H. (1984).

8.   The Difference Training Makes

The first chapter of this book showed how government sponsorship of
adult training through TOPS/OJTS was abandoned in favour of a
voluntarist approach which left market mechanisms to determine
provision for all but the long-term unemployed. One consequence of
this was a reduction in training opportunities for women, who were
particularly disadvantaged by the closure of open-entry training
courses in favour of a programme that was structured around
unemployment.   In justification for the withdrawal of public
investment, the government argued that centrally funded and planned
provision was of its nature wasteful and inefficient, and Chapter Five
suggested that this allegation derived its strength more from an
ideologically based faith in the virtues of the free market than from
any evidence that TOPS/OJTS was ineffective.

Support for the effectiveness of TOPS/OJTS can be found
throughout this book. The evidence includes long-term placement
rates in work and 'in trade', in jobs directly relevant to the skills
learned; it also embraces the patterns of occupational change that
followed training. We have seen how women who had never sat
examinations before obtained recognised vocational qualifications,
how housewives who had been away from work for many years gained
the confidence to apply for jobs, how part-time workers switched to
full-time work, and how earnings increased.   High levels of
satisfaction with the courses have been reported, and women have
been quoted who felt that training had been crucially important for
them.   Yet it still has not been proved conclusively that training made
a difference.   Those who believe that government provision is bound
to be less effective than market provision could still maintain that
women who went on TOPS/OJTS would have done well anyway,
regardless of any government scheme.

The sceptic's argument goes something like this: women who get
themselves enrolled on training courses have more motivation, more

enterprise and probably more ability than other women, and these qualities would ensure their success in the world of work whether the opportunity of training were there or not. In the academic literature this is known as the problem of 'selection effects', and the issue is a difficult one for any evaluation study to deal with. Some researchers claim that it is only possible to tell definitively whether a programme of social intervention makes any difference to the people who take part by running a social experiment, whereby clients are allocated randomly to groups who take part in the programme and groups which do not. They regard it as unfortunate that, in the field of social policy, political realities usually make it impossible even to consider random allocation as a method of deciding who gets a place and who is left out.[1]

In response to this argument it could be said that good motivation on the part of trainees is essential to the success of any training scheme. Random allocation will not give a fair test if it means that people end up getting training who did not particularly want it in the first place.[2] Indeed some would contend that one of the things wrong with schemes like Employment Training is that they are clogged up with people who want a job, not training, and are unwilling conscripts to vocational education. Many tutors on the former Youth Training Scheme could have recounted tales that underlined the force of this point.[3]

The line that was taken in the Evaluation Study represented a compromise between these two sets of arguments. On the one hand it was acknowledged that random allocation did not make much sense in the context of TOPS/OJTS and was in any case impossible to carry out. On the other hand it was felt to be important to be able to make some comparisons between people who had been on training courses and people with similar work histories who had not done so. Such a comparison may not answer all the questions that we had about the effectiveness of the programme, but it would give us substantially more information than we had before.

The comparison study

For these reasons a comparison study was built into the evaluation of TOPS/OJTS. Its purpose was to determine whether there were any differences between trainees and men and women who had not had recent training but were similar in other relevant respects on measures that represented different aspects of their experience in the labour market. Three measures were selected for examination: the chances of getting work, the degree of job satisfaction, and the level of earnings.

The method adopted was to locate a national comparison sample of people who had not recently received skills training, which was matched as closely as possible to the sample of TOPS/OJTS trainees. It was never envisaged that it would be feasible to achieve a match so good that it would be possible to rely on simple comparisons between the trainee and comparison samples - the practical problems of exact matching were far too great for this to be a viable strategy. Instead, an essential part of the design was the use of multivariate statistical modelling, for this enabled many of the other differences that were bound to be found between the trainees and the non-trainees to be taken into account. The aim was to match initially on basic variables and so reduce the differences between the two samples to the lowest achievable minimum, then to collect information on as many other factors as possible that might affect the outcome as far as jobs were concerned, and finally to control for all these variables (including the matching variables) by means of statistical modelling. This strategy gave us a good chance of detecting any effects which could be attributed to training.[4]

To identify an appropriate comparison group some method of screening had to be used. Screening is expensive, and consequently the number of criteria for selecting the comparison group had to be restricted. The criteria chosen were age, sex, employment history, and, when numbers permitted, region. Employment history is a very powerful predictor of future employment chances, and it is also probably the best single proxy for a whole range of factors that are related to employment chances but are difficult to measure by survey methods, such as motivation and interview technique. Its relevance to the evaluation was subsequently confirmed by Model 1 (see Chapter Five and Appendix Two), for this showed that, amongst all the variables investigated, the one which had the strongest association with the speed with which trainees found work after training was how long they had been unemployed beforehand.

The procedure for screening and matching the comparison group is described in Appendix One. In short, it involved brief interviews with a very large national random sample of the population in which questions were asked about their employment position in 1986. From this very large sample a smaller subsample was selected for the comparison group interview. Seven hundred and sixty usable interviews were achieved in the comparison sample, distributed, like the trainees, across all regions of Great Britain.

Given the practical difficulties of the screening process, the match between the trainee and comparison samples was surprisingly successful. Appendix One has the details. Fifty-two per cent of the trainee sample were men compared to 53 per cent of the comparison sample; 43 per cent of trainees were aged 35 or more compared to 47 per cent of the comparison group. Moreover, the matching of employment histories, which was the most ambitious part of the research design, came off surprisingly well, especially for men. When plotted over the whole period from January 1980 up until training began in 1986, the traces of the proportions of male trainees and non-trainees who were in work, unemployed, and in full-time education were very similar in shape.

Constructing a matched comparison sample for women trainees proved more difficult. There was no difficulty in locating the right number of women who were in work in 1986 or who described themselves as unemployed in that year; rather the problem concerned women who described themselves as economically inactive. Full-time housewives had almost always embarked on their TOPS/OJTS course with the intention of returning to work afterwards. In the screening for the comparison group a question was asked on whether women who were full-time housewives in 1986 had been looking for work then, but not enough such women were located to provide a proper match with trainees. As a result trainees who were economically inactive up until 1986 were bound to be more likely to get work than economically inactive members of the comparison sample, as there was no particular reason for supposing that the non-trainees wanted to return to work. This is a not a problem when we are testing the contribution of training to job satisfaction and earnings, as both of these analyses use data only for women who had been in work since 1986, but it does affect the analysis of employment chances. In consequence, we should expect training to appear to have a bigger effect on women's employment chances than on men's.

Measuring the 'training effect'

If testing the effect of training on the three outcome measures (employment chances, job satisfaction and earnings) relied on simple comparisons between the trainee and comparison samples, the validity of the test would be vulnerable to differences between the two samples that played no part in the matching process - for example, trainees might have better educational qualifications or fewer family commitments. Moreover, the initial matching could break down when subsamples were selected. Thus to measure the 'training effect', statistical models were fitted to the data. These incorporated a wide range of factors which functioned as controlling variables on the relationship of training with the outcome measures. The idea was to see how much of this relationship could be explained away by other differences between the two samples. If, after controlling for as many relevant factors as possible, training still had a significant positive association with employment probabilities, job satisfaction and earnings, conclusions about the effectiveness of training could be upheld with more confidence.

The controlling variables selected covered the demand for labour in the local labour market as measured by the unemployment rate in the local travel-to-work area in January 1987, measures of individual employment history (months spent in work in 1980 to 1985, and months spent unemployed in 1985), the type of work trainees had last done before their course and which members of the comparison sample were doing (or had last done) in 1986, age, membership of an ethnic minority group, disabilities or health problems, marital status, number of dependent children, having a child under five, being a lone parent, educational qualifications, and age of leaving full-time education. More precise definitions can be found in Appendix Two.

Throughout the 1980s anyone with a history of unemployment had a non-negligible chance of taking part, at some time or other, in a government special scheme for the unemployed. Because one of the criteria used in the matching process was past unemployment, care had to be taken not to underestimate the effects of TOPS/OJTS by unwittingly including in the comparison sample people who had received training in recent years, either on TOPS/OJTS or on other programmes. Two steps were taken to avoid this. Firstly, all members of the comparison sample (32 in all) who took part in any government scheme for the unemployed at any time from January 1986 to March

1987 inclusive were left out. 'Government scheme' was defined very broadly here, to include the Community Programme, which though primarily a job creation scheme could sometimes incorporate training, and the Youth Training Scheme, as well as designated adult training programmes. Thus while every member of the trainee sample received skills training on a government scheme between January 1986 and March 1987, no-one in the comparison sample did so. Secondly, as a fail-safe measure, the number of months which members of either sample had spent in full-time education or training between January 1980 and December 1985 was calculated, and this was used as a further control variable in the analysis.

Effects of training on employment chances

The first outcome measure to look at is employment chances. There are many ways in which these might be assessed, and in exploratory analyses several variants were tried and were found to lead to essentially the same conclusions. The measure that is reported here is a binary variable, namely whether or not the respondent was in work at all between April 1987 and September 1987 inclusive, September 1987 being the date at which interviews with trainees began. The starting point of April 1987 was chosen because it allowed at least three months for trainees to look for jobs after the end of their courses; extending the period during which employment was recorded through the six months up to September allowed additional time for trainees in more specialised areas to obtain work. The chosen period also seemed to give a fair comparison with the comparison sample, who were selected on the basis of their employment situation in 1986: by April 1987 the proportion of the comparison sample in work was increasing steadily.[5]

The question, then, was whether, after taking into account all the relevant differences that it was possible to measure between people who went on TOPS/OJTS and people who did not, the receipt of training was significantly associated with better employment chances subsequently. To test this, statistical models were fitted to predict the odds of employment for women (Model 4) and men (Model 5), odds being an alternative way of expressing probabilities. These models are given in Appendix Two. They confirmed the effectiveness of training for both sexes.

Let us look first at the results for women. As expected, a number of the control variables were associated with employment chances. Other things being equal, the probability of being in work during the period April to September 1987 was significantly reduced for older women, for women who were disabled or in ill health, and for women who had a child under five, and was significantly increased for women who had spent more time in work between 1980 and 1985. There was also a surprising finding, that when other factors were held constant, women with three or more dependent children were more likely to be in work than women with no children. As the effect of having a child under five was controlled separately, this result is probably due to women who had completed their families who, with their youngest child at school, were ready to return to work.

The principal interest, however, lies in whether, when all these factors were held constant, the employment chances of trainees were any better than those of members of the comparison sample. In fact there remained a large and highly significant difference. The odds of employment were estimated to be 2.21 times greater for women who had been on TOPS/OJTS than they were for other women.[6] This result was statistically significant beyond the .01 level of probability, which means that the probability of it occurring by chance was less than one in a hundred.

However we expected to get a result in favour of training because of the problems of finding enough women for the comparison sample who had been out of the labour market in 1986 but had expressed an intention to return to work. It was therefore important to check whether the results were equally favourable to training in the case of men, where this problem in matching did not arise.

For men, some of the variables that were significantly related to the probability of being in work were the same as for women, and others were different. The probability was reduced by a high unemployment rate locally, a past history of unemployment, age, membership of a minority ethnic group, disabilities or health problems, and having a child under five. It was increased by having spent more time in work between 1980 and 1985, by coming from a managerial or professional job, by having continued in full-time education until the age of 17-19, and by having spent some time in training between 1980 and 1985. However the effect of participation in TOPS/OJTS was even bigger for men than for women: training was estimated to increase the odds of employment by a factor of 2.72, a result significant well beyond the .001 level of probability. The fact that a positive effect was also observed for men strongly suggests that the effect of training on the employment chances of women was real, and not just an artefact of the way that the comparison group was chosen.

What do these results mean when expressed in terms of the probability of employment rather than in terms of the somewhat less familiar concept of odds? We can illustrate this by looking at some hypothetical 'typical' men and women. Take first a woman, married with one or two children (none under five) who had left school at 16 with qualifications below A Level standard and had last worked in a clerical or related job. Let us suppose that her age was the mean age for all women in the combined trainee and comparison sample (35 years and six months), that she lived in an area with the average unemployment rate (13.26 per cent), and that the number of months she had spent unemployed, in work and in training was the same as the mean for the sample. Let us further suppose that she was not a member of an ethnic minority group and had no disability or health problem. If a woman like this had no training, then under the model her predicted probability of employment in the period April to September 1987 was 80 per cent. Going on TOPS/OJTS increased her probability of employment from 80 to 90 per cent. If she were aged 50 her probability of employment would be 68 per cent without training and 82 per cent with training, and if she were only 20, the probabilities would be 89 per cent and 94 per cent respectively.

The effect on men was even greater. Take, for example, a married man with no children who had left school at 16 with no qualifications and had last worked in a manual job in manufacturing industry, and suppose that he was not a member of an ethnic minority group and had no disability or health problem. Suppose that on other variables his score was the same as the mean for all men in the combined trainee and control samples. If such a man had not been on TOPS/OJTS during 1986 his predicted probability of being in work in the period April to September 1987 was 69 per cent; getting training increased his chances to 86 per cent. If this man had been unemployed throughout 1985, training would increase his employment chances from 43 per cent to 68 per cent, an increase of 25 per cent.

The robustness of these findings was tested by fitting a variety models with different specifications, and all of these showed a very significant training effect. In addition a further series of models was fitted to a more tightly restricted subsample of the data, which excluded from the comparison sample anyone who had been on any adult training scheme of any kind since 1980. These gave essentially the same results as the models fitted to the larger data sets.

Effects of training on job satisfaction

It is vital in a modern economy that women are encouraged to make use of their skills in paid employment, and it is crucial for women's financial independence and security that those who want or need to work should be able to find jobs. However economic considerations are not the only ones that matter: it is also important that both women and men should enjoy what they do, and find it worthwhile. This in return has economic benefits: a workforce which scores highly on job satisfaction is likely to be both more stable and more productive than one whose psychological rewards are low. Thus the second outcome measure on which the Evaluation Study sought to examine the effects of adult skills training was job satisfaction.

There was already reason to believe that TOPS/OJTS had a positive effect on satisfaction with work. An earlier study of men training in manual crafts in skill centres had concluded that, 'Those who succeeded in getting and keeping jobs "in trade" were thoroughly pleased with the interest and involvement they found in their new work, and this is clearly the most important benefit of the training courses'.[7] As we have seen in Chapter Three, in the Evaluation Study the pride and delight of many women in their own achievements was equally evident, as was the renewal of their confidence in themselves. Were they, as a result, more satisfied with the work they found than other women?

With this in mind, people who were in a job at the time they were interviewed were asked how satisfied they felt with their job as a whole. The permitted responses ranged from 'very satisfied' to 'very dissatisfied'.[8] To test whether having done a TOPS/OJTS course made any difference to job satisfaction, a model was fitted to predict the odds of giving the response 'very satisfied' rather than any other response. This analysis was based only on people who were in work at the time they were interviewed; hence no difficulties arose from the failure to find enough women for the comparison sample who had not been in work in 1986 but had been seeking work at that time. The model for women (Model 6) is given in Appendix Two.

Although the model included the same controlling variables as Models 4 and 5, the factors that were related to job satisfaction were rather different from those that were related to employment chances. When other things were held constant, women were substantially more likely to be 'very satisfied' if they were married - presumably because they had more choice over whether or not to go out to work - and if they were a lone parent - perhaps because they appreciated the company more. Apart from this, having children reduced the likelihood of job satisfaction, and one might speculate that the strains imposed by combining work and family could be a factor here. Only one other of the controlling variables was significantly related to job satisfaction: women who had continued in full-time education to the age of 20 or more were less likely to say they were very satisfied than women who left school at 16. Amongst trainees, these were the women who were most likely to have experienced downward occupational mobility.

However our interest centres on the impact of adult skills training. Once more, the results were very favourable: women who had been on TOPS/OJTS and were using their new skills in their current job had odds of being very satisfied which were 2.32 times the odds for members of the comparison sample, which was significant at beyond the .01 level of probability. What is more, the effect of training was entirely confined to women who were using the skills in which they had trained - the effect for women trainees working out of trade, though positive, fell well short of statistical significance.

The results for men (Model 7 in Appendix Two) were equally favourable. In their case, only two of the controlling variables were significantly associated with job satisfaction (lone parenthood increased the odds and educational qualifications reduced them), but men who had done a TOPS/OJTS course and were using their skills in their job had odds of being very satisfied with their job which were 3.5 times as great as the odds for men in the comparison sample. Once more, there was no significant effect for men who had done a course but had failed to find a job 'in trade'.

Effects of training on earnings

The third outcome measure selected was earnings. This is regarded by many economists as a critical indicator of the value of a person's labour to the economy, and it was far from irrelevant to trainees of both sexes.

For people who were in work at the time they were interviewed, current earnings were used. Those who were not in work at that time were asked about their earnings in their last job. For members of the trainee sample this information was only used if that job had been started after the end of the training course, and for members of the comparison sample it was used only if the job had continued until April 1987 or later. Thus the information for both samples referred to comparable dates.[9] Gross hourly earnings were calculated and uprated by the Index of Average Earnings in the manner described in the last chapter, though in this instance the uprating was done to October 1988 rather than October 1987 values, in line with the later interview date for the comparison sample.

Chapter Seven examined the pattern of gains and losses in women's earnings before and after training. In this chapter we are concerned not with changes in earnings, but with their level, and the question is whether there was any significant difference between the earnings of trainees and the earnings of members of the comparison sample, when a range of other factors that affect earning power were held constant. Unlike the model for earnings change, these did not include the level of previous earnings. It had seemed reasonable to ask trainees about their earnings in their last job before they went on their course, despite the known problems with retrospective data, for the course represented a decision point in their lives and the chances were that they would have a reasonably clear recollection of their situation at that time. There was no comparable decision point in the lives of the comparison sample, and so no question was asked on previous earnings.

Model 8 in Appendix Two is the regression model that was fitted to women's earnings. According to this model, current earnings were significantly reduced for women who had experienced recent unemployment and increased for women with longer work experience since 1980. In addition, women who had been in managerial or professional jobs in 1986 (or had last worked in such jobs) had significantly higher earnings than women who had been in clerical or commercial jobs, and women with qualifications to A Level standard or better also enjoyed substantially better earnings. The family circumstances which were associated with job satisfaction were however unrelated to the level of earnings. One other factor closely approached statistical significance: as the level of unemployment in the local labour market rose, so the level of women's earnings fell.

When all these factors were held constant, the association between training and women's earnings was very marked. The earnings of women who had been on TOPS/OJTS but were in jobs which did not use the skills in which they had trained were not significantly different from the earnings of women in the comparison sample, but women who had been on TOPS/OJTS and were working 'in trade' earned an estimated 83 pence more per hour than members of the comparison sample.

However the relationship between training and earnings was more complex than this, for there was a highly significant interaction between training and educational qualifications. In effect, having educational qualifications of A Level standard or above entirely eliminated the earnings premium attributable to training. In addition, women trainees with this level of qualifications who were working out of trade lost the advantage that their qualifications should have given them. The explanation for this is not hard to find if we remember the patterns of gains and losses that were described in the last chapter and the occupational changes that underlay these changes in earnings. Women without formal qualifications usually sought training in order to get access to more attractive and better paid jobs; women who were already well qualified often sought training because they could not or did not wish to continue in the kind of work which they had done before. As a result, in many cases they earned less after training than they had earned before.[10]

One of the most important reasons why the earnings of women trainees were higher than the earnings of women in the comparison sample was probably that, as long as they were able to find work relevant to their training, going on a training course considerably mitigated the adverse effect of taking a career break on the earnings of women returners. The 'Women and Employment' study, a very important national investigation of women's employment patterns conducted in 1980, established that women returners often experienced downward occupational mobility, especially if they had been away from work for a number of years and especially if they returned to work part-time. Forty-four per cent of women who had been away from work for more than a year after the birth of their first child who returned to part-time work went back to a job at a lower occupational level than they had been working at before.[11] This was bound to have an adverse effect on their rates of pay.

The association between taking a career break and lower earnings was also found for women in the Evaluation Study, and is shown in Model 8 by the significant positive association between earnings and the amount of time spent in work between 1980 and 1985. Indeed, the proportion of women who had recently gone back to work after a career break was higher in the trainee than in the comparison sample: 26 per cent of women trainees for whom earnings data are available did not work at all in 1985, the year before they started their course, compared to 21 per cent of women in the comparison sample. This alone should lead us to expect that the earnings of trainees would be lower. However the difference between the earnings of women who had not worked at all in 1985 and women who had worked for the whole of that year was much wider for members of the comparison sample than it was for trainees. Table 8.1 shows that for women who had been on TOPS/OJTS there was very little difference between the mean earnings of those who had been in work for the whole of 1985, the year before their courses took place, and those who had been away from work for the whole of that year, with the former earning on average eight pence per hour more than the latter. In contrast, in the comparison sample the difference in earnings between these two groups of women was quite big - a gap of 67 pence.[12] This adds to the by now quite considerable evidence that adult training served a very important function in enabling women to re-enter the labour market at a level much closer to the level at which they had left.

As with employment chances and job satisfaction, it was not only women whom training helped to improve their earnings. The results for men are given in Model 9 in Appendix Two.[13] Men earned considerably more than women, regardless of whether they received training, but the pattern of relationships between earnings and the controlling variables was similar in many respects to the pattern for women. Earnings were higher for men who spent more time in work since 1980 and who had educational qualifications of A Level standard or above, and they were lower for men who lived in localities with

Table 8.1 Earnings and career breaks: women who went on TOPS/OJTS compared with members of the comparison sample

	trainee sample	comparison sample
Mean gross hourly earnings in current job[1]:		
(a) in work for the whole of 1985	£3.43	£3.34
(N)	(96)	(86)
(b) away from work for the whole of 1985	£3.35	£2.67
(N)	(82)	(51)
difference between (a) and (b)	£0.08	£0.67

1   Or, for those not currently in work, the most recent job, provided this was after the TOPS/OJTS course (trainees) or continued to April 1987 or later (comparison sample).

Source: Evaluation Study.

high unemployment rates and for men who had previously worked in low skill service occupations.

On the main question at issue, the analysis produced exactly the same results for men as it had done for women. When all the controlling variables were held constant, there was no significant difference in earnings between men in the comparison sample and men who had been on TOPS/OJTS but were working out of trade. In contrast, trainees who were in jobs which used the skills in which they had trained were predicted by the model to earn significantly more than members of the comparison sample - an estimated premium of 139 pence per hour.

This, however, was not the end of the story about men's earnings, for there was also a significant interaction between training and age and between training and educational qualifications. Men in the age groups 35-44 and 45 plus had the earnings premium associated with working 'in trade' substantially reduced, and the same was true for men with educational qualifications of A Level standard or higher. These findings suggest that, just as for women, adult skills training for men was an equalising force, enabling the young and poorly qualified to improve their earnings relative to other men, whilst providing fewer earnings gains for those who were older and better qualified. Many of these men had in fact experienced a drop in earnings after their course compared to their earnings in their last job, and many had been made redundant in the harsh economic conditions of the first half of the 1980s. For some of these men the only alternatives to accepting retraining and a possible cut in income were either long term unemployment or employment in less skilled jobs at even lower rates of pay.

Overview

In sum, the analyses based on the comparison group gave unequivocal support to the conclusion that TOPS/OJTS had a positive effect on employment chances, on job satisfaction and on earnings, and that it had this effect for both women and men. In the analysis of employment chances it obviously was not possible to distinguish between trainees who were in jobs which used their skills and trainees who were employed 'out of trade', but in the analyses of job satisfaction and earnings, where this distinction could be made, it was particularly notable that the benefits of training only accrued to trainees who were working 'in trade'. This finding adds weight to the conclusion about the benefits of training, for it suggests that the differences that were found between the trainee and comparison samples were not a product of any failure to match the two samples adequately or to control properly for other variables that might affect the three outcome measures, but were indeed due to the fact that the trainees had been on TOPS/OJTS and the members of the comparison sample had not.

Notes to Chapter Eight

1. The debate over the need for experimental designs in evaluation studies in the field of social policy has been waged particularly in America, where evaluation studies are much more common than in this country. See, for example, LaLonde 1986.
2. I am indebted to Michael White for this point.
3. In illustration of this, D. Lee *et al*. (1990) give a depressing account of what it can be like trying to teach a group of bored teenagers on the Youth Training Scheme who cannot see the point of what they are supposed to be doing.
4. In statistical language, the aim of the matching process was to reduce the between-sample variance on variables which were related to the outcome measures; this makes the statistical tests used to detect the 'training effect' more efficient.

5. The choice of a binary variable to summarise employment during these six months may seem perverse when it would be easy instead to use the total number of months in work during the period. The choice is dictated by the fact that the majority of respondents were either out of work for the whole period or in work for the whole period, and this was true for both the trainee and the comparison samples. The bimodal nature of the distribution of months spent in work meant that ordinary least squares regression techniques would have been inappropriate.

6. The effect on the odds is bigger than the effect on the probabilities, as the following example illustrates. If 67 out of 100 women in Group A are in work and 33 are not in work, then the odds of employment are 67/33, which is 2.0 or two to one, while the probability of unemployment is 67 per cent. If in Group B, also consisting of 100 women, 80 are in work and 20 are not in work, then the odds of employment are 80/20, or 4.0, or four to one, while the probability of employment is 80 per cent. Thus the odds of unemployment are twice as great for Group B as they are for Group A, but the probability of unemployment is only 13 per cent higher.

7. Berthoud, R. (1978), p.84.

8. The question was taken from the questionnaire used by the General Household Survey.

9. Just as in Chapter Seven, people who were self-employed were excluded from the analysis, as it was not thought possible to get reliable information about their earnings.

10. See Table 7.4 in Chapter Seven.

11. Martin, J. and Roberts, C. (1984), Table 10.17

12. Model 8 includes two terms representing the interaction between training and the length of recent work experience. Although neither of these reached significance, their inclusion has an important effect on the model, for when they are removed the main effect of being a trainee working 'in trade' loses its statistical significance. The explanation lies with women who were returning to work after a career break, as described in the text.

13. The absence of reliable information on the earnings of the self-employed meant that more men than women were lost from the analysis, and in particular, men working in the construction industry were under-represented.

9. Summary and Conclusions: The Case for Public Investment

In 1916 a Miss Constance Smith, a woman 'specially conversant with matters concerning the employment of women in consequence of the war', addressed an audience in Oxford on the topic, 'Women in industry today and tomorrow'. She spoke of:

> the adaptability and capacity women had shown to the change-over of their erstwhile occupations owing to the war. The necessities of the time had obliged them to take up new trades...A little learning had taught them that difficulty could be overcome. With the overcoming of the difficulty had come a most remarkable new sense of power. Along with the sense of power had come a new interest in work. A lot of trades were of a mind-killing nature. In the learning of new trades hundreds and thousands of women were finding out for the first time that work might be interesting...A good many girls who never had a living wage before were now earning something more than a living wage.

The success of women in keeping industry running while the men were away led her to conclude that:

> They could not expect that working women would be content to take, after the war, the very unsatisfactory position which for the most part they occupied before the war. One presumed that while from the point of view of self-interest the nation would recognise that training was due to women, as well as men, in industry in the future gratitude also would have something to say.[1]

Unhappily for Miss Smith's optimism, in 1918 the emergency training programmes which had given many women their first opportunity of learning a skill started to be closed down and replaced by rehabilitation programmes for ex-servicemen, whilst in the factories women left their jobs to make room for the returning soldiers. The Central Council on Women's Training and Employment re-directed its energies towards preparing women for employment in domestic service, and the ordinary working girl resumed her 'very unsatisfactory position' in the labour market.[2]

No-one could deny that, in the three-quarters of a century that have passed since Miss Smith gave her address, women have made enormous gains. Even so, for a long time women's vocational training remained neglected in comparison with men's. As recently as 1973 the National Council of Women gave evidence to a committee of Parliament that:

> A spokesman from the Department of Employment has recently suggested to one of our members that (a) many girls do not want training, (b) the overall employment position should be considered before training more married women; and that (c) it may not be good for the community that married women should be trained, and that the only circumstances in which more women will be trained is when there is economic need.[3]

As the new feminist movements gathered strength, official attitudes began to change. In 1976 the Manpower Services Commission's report on 'Training Opportunities for Women' recognised that there was an unsatisfied demand for training from women, and three years later a further report acknowledged the need to open up training for women in traditional masculine skills. In the same year the MSC launched the pilot of its Wider Opportunities for Women programme, financed by the European Economic Community's Social Fund, which was designed to give women the opportunity to sample work and training in a broad range of fields. By 1983 this was offering 572 places in 20 different centres. At the same time TOPS was training many thousands of women (41,000 in 1978), and courses under the TOPS umbrella designed to meet the special needs of women returners were becoming increasingly common.[4]

However, as we saw in Chapter One, the persistence of record levels of unemployment for several years in the 1980s led the government to cut progressively the funding for these programmes. In 1988 they were formally closed down, and the government's major efforts in adult training were focussed on the launch of Employment Training. Today, whether or not public funds are used to provide courses specifically designed to attract and help women is left entirely to the discretion of the employer-led Training and Enterprise Councils (or Local Enterprise Companies in Scotland). According to official policy, the prime responsibility for ensuring that women - and men -

get the training they need belongs to employers and to the individuals themselves, and the market is the mechanism through which this responsibility should be discharged.

It is the contention of this book that adult training for women cannot and should not be left solely to the market. Women's skills cannot be properly developed without planned and centrally funded efforts . The case for public investment in women's training is in part the case for justice between the sexes. Women still have many fewer opportunities than men to acquire skills when they are young. Despite the rhetoric of sexual equality, the labour market is nearly as deeply divided by gender today as it was a generation ago, and so also is vocational training. From these unequal beginnings, women lose ground still further when they form partnerships and have children, for it is still women who take most of the responsibility for caring for children. When they are ready to go back to paid employment, they have every right to a little help from the public purse in the form of training in up-to-date skills.

But justice is not the only platform on which the case for public investment in women's training rests, for the argument is as much about self-interest as justice. For a nation which has largely its wits to rely on for its survival as an advanced economy, it would be foolish indeed to overlook the potential of half the workforce. In Chapter One we saw how grossly the country wastes women's abilities. Of all women in the labour market who have degree level qualifications, only a third work in professional jobs or as employers or managers, and one in ten women with A Level GCE or equivalent qualifications is in a semi-skilled or unskilled job. It will take a lot more than adult training to enable women to reach their full potential, but training can make an important contribution. Nor should efforts be confined to training for adults, for the inadequacy of Britain's system of vocational training for young people continues to be a source of concern to educationalists and industrialists alike. This book, however, has concentrated on the particular role that adult training can play.

The Evaluation Study proved that public investment in well-planned and well-funded training for women, such as used to exist under TOPS and its successor, the Old Job Training Scheme, produces very worthwhile benefits. The findings of the study have surprised no-one who had any involvement with TOPS/OJTS; they knew that it worked well. On a recent visit to a Job Centre, the author asked two officials if they had been around when TOPS still existed. The first remembered TOPS well: 'We used to get people coming in to ask if they could go on that'. The second was even more familiar with the programme - it was doing a TOPS course that had enabled her to get the job she is in today. What people find much more surprising than the fact that adult training for women is effective is the fact that the argument for public investment in women's training should need to be spelled out with such care.

Women's need for training

It is no part of this argument to deny that men also can benefit enormously from adult training, or that meeting their training needs should not also be a goal of public policy. However, recent policy developments have led to women's needs becoming relatively more neglected than those of men. It would probably be unfair to suggest that this neglect is deliberate; it appears to have arisen because the consequences of recent shifts in government training policy have not been thought through with regard to women. Current policy stresses the prime responsibility of employers - but employers have always invested more in training men than training women. Current policy maintains that individuals should fund the development of their own careers - but men are generally in a much stronger position financially to do this. Current policy says that public finance should be largely reserved for training the long-term unemployed - but men who are without a job are much more likely to satisfy the criteria for long-term unemployment than are jobless women.

One group for whom opportunities have been notably reduced since the demise of TOPS/OJTS are women returners. As private childcare is expensive and public childcare extremely scarce, a lot of women have no option but to give up paid employment while their children are small. Even if childcare were more widely available, many women would still choose to look after their children full-time. Other women are forced to stay at home to care for sick or elderly relatives. Yet often the penalty for taking on these responsibilities is not just a few years wages foregone, a few years longer to wait for promotion, but a permanent move down to lower skilled work than was done before. Women who have been away from work for some years can gain enormously from refresher courses which enable them to re-enter work at a level close to the level at which they left. Others, especially if they have been away from work for many years, may never regain the confidence to go back to work at all were it not for courses run by people who are sympathetic to their needs and who have the skill and experience to rebuild their faith in their own abilities. For women like this training can be a kind of stepping stone between the home and the world of work.

Training can also serve a very important function for women who have already returned to work following a career break. Many such women have moved down the occupational ladder from skilled white collar jobs as clerks, typists or secretaries, into jobs as canteen assistants, cleaners, check-out operators and other types of work where pay and conditions are poorer and the level of skill demanded is not very great. They are obliged to take such jobs by a combination of factors. Some have skills which have become rusty with disuse; some have skills which have been overtaken by new technologies and which need updating. Others may still have good skills, but have lost confidence. Often low skill jobs are taken as a short-term expedient because the hours or location fit in with family commitments, but they can become a trap from which it is very difficult to escape. Working at a low skill level makes the problem of decaying skills and confidence even worse, and low wages mean that women cannot afford childcare and the other facilities that they need if they are to give more of their time to paid employment. From the employer's point of view, such women are a cheap and dispensable workforce in which they are unlikely to be willing to invest. The Evaluation Study showed that access to training can enable women to break out of this trap and climb back up the ladder to the skill level at which they were employed before their career break.

Current policy makes little provision for women like this. When ET was first launched, some places were created for returners, but to qualify for one of these the trainee had to have been away from work for more than two years. Women who had already gone back to work, albeit to a lower skilled job than they did before, were not eligible. Now that ET is itself in a state of flux, no-one can say what provision the TECs will make for returners. Let us hope that the new flexibility over eligibility requirements for ET will be seen by the TECs as an opportunity to broaden the range of clients for whom they cater. One of the great merits of TOPS/OJTS was that it was open to all, regardless of whether they were in work or not, as long as the applicant had a serious interest in getting training. Thus it was able to cater for training needs arising in many different ways, without formal rules excluding many from eligibility.

It is, of course, not only career break women who may need training or retraining in adulthood. As we saw in Chapter Two, women who lose their jobs through redundancy or other causes may find at times of high unemployment that it is only through training that they are able to regain a foothold in employment, and women who took jobs with no training when they were young may regard training in adulthood as a second chance for achieving personal fulfilment. In other cases the catalyst is a crisis of some kind: divorce or the death of a partner, leaving the woman the sole breadwinner; leaving a job and moving house in response to the demands of the husband's work; illness or injury which makes it impossible to pursue the career which was chosen first. It is impossible to foresee all the circumstances in which the need for training or retraining may arise, and in this lies the value of an open training programme, where need is self-defined.

However good a country's system of vocational education for young people, there will always be a role to be played by a well-developed system of adult training, particularly at times of rapid industrial and technological change. In Britain, however, the need for adult training is greater because initial vocational training is poor compared to many other advanced industrial nations. Vocational training in Germany, for example, is more extensive, more structured, and better certificated than in Britain, and the formal structure and wide recognition of vocational qualifications make it much less likely that people who possess vocational qualifications will be employed at a level below the level to which they have been trained. As a result, women returners appear to be much less likely to experience downward occupational mobility than women in Britain.[5]

The motivation for adult training usually springs from economic necessity, but there were also women on TOPS/OJTS who had earned a good salary but had been unhappy in their job. Re-training was not usually undertaken just on a whim; it usually entailed quite arduous study and loss of income whilst the trainee re-established herself in a new career. As a result, the number of women who sought training for this reason was small. Nevertheless the right to change career is particularly important for women, because their initial career choices are more constrained than men's, and are made at an age when there is maximum pressure to conform to gender stereotypes. Indeed, the contemplation of a new career should be encouraged in an economy which has a shortage of skills in the 'masculine' technologies, and whose need for a flexible workforce is frequently stressed.

The role of evaluation

Whatever policies are adopted on training, it is essential that they be subjected to regular monitoring and evaluation, and that the results should be fully in the public domain. Evaluation research is, however, notably under-developed in Britain, particularly in comparison with the USA, and the results of monitoring exercises have not always been published as quickly as they might. Thus, for example, although follow-up surveys of ET trainees began in summer 1989, first results were not published until late in 1990.

Evaluation is not easy. Any large-scale programme impinges on the world in complex ways, and needs to be assessed from many points of view. The Evaluation Study which this book describes itself ignores some very important aspects of TOPS/OJTS: for example, it says nothing about the selection process for entry to the programme, or about the extent and nature of dropout. What is more, it is rare that a programme has just one goal, and it may be more successful in pursuing some goals than others. But the difficulty of proper evaluation should not deter us from the attempt. Our strategy should be to seek evidence of more than one kind, from more than one source, and in relation to more than one possible effect. No single piece of evidence will be conclusive, but in the composite picture we will approach nearer to the truth.

The effectiveness of adult skills training for women

As regards the effectiveness of adult skills training for women on TOPS/OJTS, the Evaluation Study, which was based on a nationally representative sample of trainees, collected evidence of the way in which they rated their training, their experiences after leaving, what they said in their own words about the impact of training on their lives, and how they progressed compared to women who had not had training. It also examined several different consequences of participation: qualifications gained, the probability of getting a job, movements from part-time to full-time work, earnings, skills used, occupational mobility, and job satisfaction. The evidence consistently pointed to one conclusion: that training was generally very worthwhile. It worth at this point summarising the main elements in this evidence.

Chapter Three reported the high levels of satisfaction that women expressed with their training. Though the majority obtained useful qualifications on their courses, many also pointed to personal gains which could not be measured so easily, and in particular, to the growth of confidence in themselves and their abilities. Chapter Five followed women after they had finished training. It showed that although placement rates in jobs were good three months after training, they were substantially better in the long-term, with 82 per cent of women trainees in work more than two years after the end of their course. What is more, four-fifths of those in work were in jobs which made direct use of the skills in which they had trained. Although women who had been in work in the month before their course were more likely to find employment than women who had not been in work then, women who had been away from work for a very long time were just as likely to get work after training as those whose absence had been of only short duration. Nearly two-thirds of all women's jobs after training were full-time, and 45 per cent of women who had been working part-time before their course moved into full-time work afterwards. The statistical modelling described in Chapter Five also showed that gaining a recognised qualification on their course helped trainees to get a job that used their new skills, and suggested that appropriate training leading to a recognised qualification may go some way towards reducing the disadvantage in the labour market experienced by older workers and members of ethnic minorities.

Chapter Six compared the jobs that women got after their course with the jobs that they had been doing previously. The proportion in clerical and related jobs increased from 46 to 85 per cent, while the proportion in sales occupations or low skilled personal service work fell from 38 per cent to five per cent. Often women who moved from this kind of work into higher grade white collar jobs had done clerical or secretarial work some years previously, but had experienced downward occupational mobility on their return to work after a career break. There was also a net movement out of semi-skilled and unskilled jobs in manufacturing, such as packing or repetitive assembly, and into better paid jobs which demanded more skill, such as sewing machining. Movements between industries before and after training underlined these patterns. The chapter also investigated the motivations of the large number of women who had been clerical or related workers and who returned to the same type of work after their course. Two thirds of these had been away from work before their course, and many of this group wanted refresher courses or better qualifications to help them get a job. The third who had been in employment before starting their course generally were seeking additional skills (such as word processing or shorthand) to widen the range of jobs that were open to them and increase their earning power.

Chapter Seven looked at the impact of training on earnings. Overall women's earnings after training were 11 pence per hour higher than they were before, and 58 per cent of women increased their earnings by at least five pence per hour. Mean gains would have been greater were it not for a small number of women who had previously been in well paid professional, semi-professional or managerial jobs who had entered training as the first step towards a new career. The biggest gains were made by women who were able to exchange a low-skill job in the service sector for a clerical or related post, and generally, the lower the level of earnings before the course, the greater was the improvement afterwards.

Finally, Chapter Eight brought into consideration a comparison sample of people whose work histories had been similar to those of trainees before they started their courses, but who had not received training. Multivariate statistical modelling based on the two samples indicated that training on TOPS/OJTS significantly increased the chances of finding employment, and women in work were significantly more likely to be very satisfied with their job if they had received training. Other things being equal, women who had been on TOPS/OJTS and who subsequently found a job using the skills in which they had trained were estimated to earn 83 pence per hour more than women who had not had recent training, and there was evidence that training considerably mitigated the generally detrimental effect of a career break on earnings.

Taken together, this evidence confirmed what many people already knew to be the case, namely that high quality adult training 'off-the-job' in the TOPS/OJTS style has very positive effects for women.

Is training women as worthwhile as training men?

Despite the advances of recent years, women are still commonly regarded by employers as an unreliable source of labour compared to men, and not worth as much investment in training. The findings of the Evaluation Study demonstrate that training for women is every bit as worthwhile as training for men. After their courses women found work more quickly than men did, and their long-term placement rates were very similar to men's. In addition, more women than men found jobs that used the skills in which they had trained, and more women than men improved their earnings after their course compared to what they had been earning before.

For women returners in particular, training can often establish a virtuous circle. Improved skills, qualifications and confidence increase their chances of getting a job with good pay and conditions on their re-entry to the labour market, and these increased rewards to employment in turn increase the chances that the return to work will be permanent.[6] Good wages can go a long way towards reducing the strains imposed on women who combine family and paid employment, by enabling them to afford better quality child care and labour saving devices, and by raising the importance attached by their partners and children to their employment.

The inadequacy of women's training opportunities

The first chapter of this book showed how recent trends in government policy towards adult training had led to a decline in government spending on women relative to spending on men. This was not a result of deliberate discrimination against women, but was rather a side effect of the closure of TOPS/OJTS, where training was available to all who felt the need, and the concentration of funding on ET, where eligibility depends largely on long-term registered unemployment. It is one of the tasks of social scientists to point out the unintended consequences of such shifts in policy.

The government's policy that the costs of adult training must be borne primarily by employers and individuals without public subsidy will almost inevitably reduce opportunities for women. However irrationally, employers still tend to regard women employees as a risk, and do not provide as much training for them as they do for men. Training for women returners, who have yet to prove their commitment to the labour market, is viewed as even more of a gamble.

This attitude towards women returners was evident in some of the case studies from the Evaluation Study, in that returners who had been out of the labour market for a long time could find that they had to 'prove' themselves in a job somewhat below the level of their abilities, before they could move into the jobs they were really suited to. Furthermore, employers will never be persuaded to pay for the training of the women who perhaps benefited most from TOPS/OJTS: these were the women who sought training because it enabled them to move out of low skilled jobs into better rewarded posts with a different employer.

The stress on the responsibility of individuals to take care of their own training has been made even more prominent in the government's most recent statement of its position on training. The Secretary of State for Employment has headed this statement with the following words:

> Perhaps our most formidable challenge is the need to increase motivation among our people, to change antiquated attitudes and values, to instil a philosophy of self-development and self-investment in every worker.[7]

Later he spells out what this entails:

> We must raise the awareness and motivation of individuals so that they are more willing to train and to take personal responsibility for their own development... Individuals need to be motivated to invest some of their own time and, where appropriate, money in training.[8]

This policy, which we might term the 'bootstrap' theory of training, seems particularly unhelpful to women. The low level of women's hourly pay - still on average only two-thirds the pay of men[9] - together with the fact that many women can only work part-time makes it unlikely that they will have the independent financial resources to pay for their own training. To finance training, many would have to go into debt, and the very low take-up figures for women reported in Chapter One for the government's Career Development Loans prove that this is a viable option only for a very few. To incur large personal debts is a very risky strategy, as the huge rise in the number of debt defaulters following the expansion of personal credit during the 1980s has proved. Women would be justified in putting their own financial position and that of their families at risk only if they could be sure of secure and well paid employment afterwards. Women's family commitments, and the casualised nature of much of the employment that is open to them, mean that their expectations can never be as confident in this regard as men's.

Public versus private provision

One important finding of the Evaluation Study was that the concept of 'training for stock', for the general needs of the economy rather than for a specific job with a particular employer, was vindicated by the long-term placement rates of trainees. Though occasionally it took some time for things to come right for a trainee, he or she - and the economy - usually reaped the benefit of training in the end. This fact is relevant to the question of whether public investment in adult training can be justified, for 'training for stock' means training for the general public good, not only for the benefit of particular individuals or employers.

The government accepts that the state has a responsibility to provide education and training for young people, despite the fact that both individuals and employers benefit from this. Its policy on adult training is inconsistent with this. As one commentator has put it, 'Why should youth training require massive public expenditure and a policy of training for stock, and adult training merit neither, if both are seen to be vital for future economic growth?'[10] This is not the only inconsistency in the government's position. Why should the personal returns to training justify insisting that individuals fund it themselves, if training 'for stock' is wasteful? Individuals who finance their own training are effectively training for stock, in that they rely on finding work with a future unknown employer to get a return on their investment. The question is thus not whether training for stock is a good policy, but whether the private or public purse should pay for it. If the country needs skills as badly as the government says it does, it must be wrong that the costs of creating those skills should fall heavily on private individuals.

What then, of the argument that the most efficient way to provide training to match the country's skills needs is through market mechanisms? To date, the market has proved itself singularly inadequate to meet this challenge. A historical survey of industrial training in Britain leads to the conclusion that voluntarism alone has proved unable to generate the training opportunities that the national economy so patently requires.[11] There is no reason in principle why a publicly funded training programme should be inefficient, and public funding is perfectly compatible with decentralised planning and delivery. The government's own figures on placement rates for TOPS/OJTS in the 1980s give evidence of the effectiveness of that particular programme. Though placement rates slumped in the recession of 1980/81, they recovered very quickly, long before unemployment nationally stopped rising. In order to achieve this, those involved in the programme must have had some success in determining the nature and location of skills shortages that were persisting in the recession, and in planning provision accordingly.

If one wished to be cynical, one might argue that there is a 'catch 22' in government policy on adult training. If a publicly funded programme is ineffective, then (quite rightly) it is to be scrapped, but if it is effective, and enables trainees to find work and increase their earnings, then the policy says that it is also to be scrapped, for in that case employers and individuals are made to foot the bill.

It was not only ideological considerations, but also the expense of the programme that brought about the demise of TOPS/OJTS. Where women are concerned, the direct costs of training were in fact lower than for men, for (as Chapter Two showed) their courses were on average shorter. In addition, their courses were more often part-time, and consequently fewer women than men were entitled to the training allowance. Nevertheless, quality training is never cheap - the point is whether it is effective. The costs of training have to be assessed in relation to the benefits, and the benefits to the country of taking someone out of a low skill job and equipping them with the skills they need to do a job where labour is in short supply are enormous. The poor success rate of ET means that although the cost per filled place is low compared to TOPS/OJTS, when costs are calculated in relation to results, the comparison is less favourable. The most recent estimate of training costs on ET sets them at £3,500 per 'positive outcome' (i.e. per trainee in work or in full-time education or training three months after leaving).[12] Although this is undoubtedly higher than costs for TOPS/OJTS (in 1986 costs were £4,216 per completed training course), the calculation takes no account of the relatively low value of the kind of skills that are learned on ET compared to those acquired on TOPS/OJTS.

The need for quality training

It is an unhappy fact that an over-emphasis on reducing costs leads to low quality training. The change of policy had not gone unnoticed by the trainees who took part in the Evaluation Study. By the time of the postal follow-up in spring 1989 TOPS/OJTS had been closed down for nearly a year, and several expressed their regret that this was so. The following is an extract from a letter from one trainee (in this case a man), who had found his own TOPS/OJTS course first rate:

> Because the subject interests me, I have tried to keep in touch with what is happening in computer training - at least at the 'conversion' level where people switch to a new career as an analyst or programmer. What I have seen and heard is profoundly depressing. The push towards cheaper courses has led to shorter courses and to the entry into this sector of what can only be described as cowboys.'

Having given the example of a friend's experiences on one of these new courses, he concluded,

> ...it does tend to throw a poor light on government efforts to obtain better value for money per training pound invested. The quality of the personnel and the ethics of the training outfit do play a part too!

There is no doubt that much of the training provided on ET is low quality, and this is acknowledged by the TECs themselves as well as in the perceptions of the general public. Chapters Three and Five showed the consequences of this by comparing the performance of TOPS/OJTS with the results of the government's own follow-up survey of ET. Higher level training in the new technologies - a substantial element of TOPS/OJTS - represented only a minute proportion of training on ET, and training for low skill occupations was much more prominent. The number of ET trainees gaining qualifications was about a third of the figure on TOPS/OJTS, and placement rates in jobs were substantially lower for ET trainees.

During the 1980s, government training schemes have become closely identified with unemployment. The marriage has not been fruitful. It has devalued and stigmatised training, and confused the issues. There can be no doubt that many unemployed people would benefit from training, but there are also many who have no interest in training, or have already been through government training programmes and now just want a job. Skills training and job creation are not and should not attempt to serve exactly the same functions; government training schemes via their identification with unemployment have risked becoming a source of cheap labour for employers and a euphemism for workfare. The reputation of government training schemes has not always been so low, and it need not be so now. We need to re-establish their credibility by setting up programmes that give high quality training, are relevant to industrial needs without providing employers with cheap labour, and are open to all who want to make a serious commitment to learning new skills, whether unemployed or not.

A further desperate need of public training programmes is for stability and for carefully planned and monitored development. During the last decade, driven by the need to keep pace with the ever growing numbers of young and long-term unemployed, new government schemes have been launched only to disappear again within the space of a year or two. Funding arrangements were subject to even more frequent alterations. This breakneck pace of change caused confusion and chronic financial insecurity for the organisations contracted to provide the training places. In the government's scramble to find enough training places to meet its guarantees, too often a blind eye was turned to low standards of provision. Divorcing public skills training programmes from their direct association with unemployment would give them the space to develop in a rational and sustainable manner, with the focus on the nation's long-term skills needs rather than immediate political demands.

Gendered training

Chapter Four raised a fundamental problem which plagues attempts to improve the position of women in the workforce in Britain, namely the clustering of women within a narrow range of occupations traditionally regarded as 'woman's work'. These occupations are typically less well paid than the jobs done by men, and carry fewer opportunities for advancement. Training on TOPS/OJTS mirrored these divisions: women were heavily concentrated on clerical and secretarial courses and courses for 'women's' jobs in manufacturing (such as sewing machining), and extremely sparsely represented on courses in engineering science and technology and the traditional manual crafts. Though training enabled many women to move to more skilled and better paid jobs, they achieved this through traditional female career paths and not by breaking into male strongholds.

One of the reasons why so few women trained in engineering science and technology appeared to be that they lacked a basis on which to build. It was possible for a man whose academic qualifications were not high to gain entry to technological level courses in engineering if he had done a relevant apprenticeship at craft level or had several years industrial experience. As long as the lower rungs of this particular occupational ladder remain closed to women, it is more difficult for them to gain access to the higher echelons, and TOPS/OJTS made little impression on the problem. However a small number of women did train in computer programming and systems analysis and secured relevant employment afterwards. These women were nearly all young, childless and well educated. Women without good qualifications may have been deterred by lack of confidence in their logical skills, whilst the youthful age structure of the computing profession may also have disadvantaged women, who tend to be older than men when they seek training. The very few women who trained in 'masculine' skilled manual trades were in new industries such as electronics, and it may be easier for women to gain a foothold here than in old established crafts.

Sexual segregation in work, and the consequent sexual segregation of training, will not be overcome without a vigorously pursued equal opportunities programme. The fact that there are skills shortages in the newer technologies should encourage employers to increase their efforts to recruit women in these fields, but the history of the 1980s has proved that skills shortages alone are not a sufficient catalyst for change. Adult training programmes can play a part, through targeted recruitment drives, special arrangements to support women training in male-dominated fields, and efforts to persuade employers of the suitability of women for this kind of work.

Adult training for women in the 1990s
The solutions to the training problems of two decades ago are not necessarily the answers that we need to the new challenges of the 1990s. This book does not argue that TOPS/OJTS should be taken down from the shelf, dusted off, and put back in the front window. The programme had some problems of its own: there was a need to ensure that the most up-to-date practice was taught on all the courses, to integrate practical work experience with classroom learning, to get women into a wider range of fields, and to ensure that trainees received

157

the best possible guidance both before they enrolled on a course and after they had completed it.[13] Nevertheless we should build on the best elements in all the various training programmes which the last twenty years have seen, and this means examining each one on its merits, as free as possible from the distorting influence of ideology.

The two main merits of TOPS/OJTS were that it opened the door to training to everyone, and that the training it offered was of high quality and focussed on the country's emerging skills needs. There is everything to be gained by letting women and men positively choose training because they value it and recognise that they need it, and there is no way that an essentially low skill training programme like ET can create the skills base needed in a modern economy. These are the major lessons of the TOPS/OJTS programme which were forgotten when it was closed down.

Where women are concerned, the opportunities open to them to get adult training cannot be permitted to dwindle simply as an unforeseen side effect of new policies. Even worse, there is a risk that the recession of 1991 will reduce still further their remaining training opportunities. The vision of employers is notoriously short-term when it comes to planning for skills needs, and rising male unemployment could easily divert their attention from training for women. The 1988 White Paper on employment at least listed women as one of a number of potential sources of skilled labour that could be used to bridge Britain's skills gap. Two years later, the Secretary of State for Employment's 'Strategic Guidance on Training and Enterprise' did not mention women once, except in the technical 'Annex'.[14] If it is seriously intended that the 1990s are to be the 'Skills Decade', it must be made a major aim of public training policy to give women the chance to develop their skills.

Notes to Chapter Nine

1. *Oxford Chronicle*, March 3 1916.
2. Sheldrake, J. and Vickerstaff, S. (1987).
3. House of Commons Expenditure Committee (1973), quoted in Wickham, A. (1986).
4. The information in this paragraph is taken from Wickham, A. (1986).
5. König, W. (1987).

6. As evidence for this claim, L.B. Shaw (1983) conducted an analysis of a large national longitudinal study of women's work experience in the USA which showed the positive impact of additional work experience and qualifications on the probability that women returners would remain in the labour force once they had re-entered it.
7. Michael Howard, in the Preface to *1990s: The Skills Decade*, Employment Department (1990b).
8. *Ibid*, p9.
9. Labour Market Data Table 5.6, *Employment Gazette* Vol. 99 No. 2, February 1991.
10. Ryan, *Lloyds Bank Review* April 1984, quoted in J. Sheldrake and S. Vickerstaff (1987).
11. J. Sheldrake and S. Vickerstaff (1987).
12. *Hansard Written Answers*, col 384, Nov. 27 1990, quoted in Unemployment Unit and Youthaid: *Working Brief*, February 1991, p4.
13. A fuller discussion of these issues can be found in J. Payne (1989).
14. Employment Department (1990b).

Appendix One: Survey Methods

The Trainee Sample

The Evaluation Study is based on a nationally representative sample of 2,710 men and women who completed training under the Old Job Training Scheme during the second half of 1986. Basic data for this sample was collected from trainee registration forms, and a sub-sample of 785 was interviewed in September and October 1987. A further postal follow-up of this subsample took place in Spring 1989.

In early 1987 the Manpower Services Commission wrote to all of its area offices in England, Scotland and Wales instructing them to supply a prescribed number of names and addresses of trainees who had completed Old Job Training Scheme courses during the third and fourth quarters of 1986, together with basic data collected at the time they registered for courses. The targets set were designed to yield a national sample of 2,929 trainees - 7.1 per cent of 1985/86 total of 41,039 trainees - which was representative of all Old Job Training Scheme completers by region and the broad subject area of their training. In the event the names of 2,710 trainees were returned, the shortfall being partly due to the fact that the estimates of the 1985/86 population figures were out of date by the time the sample was drawn. Nevertheless the proportion of this sample in each of the 11 subject areas represented was within 0.6 per cent of the corresponding proportion in the 1985/86 population of trainees, and the proportion in each of the ten MSC regions was within 1.4 per cent of the population proportion.

All trainees selected in this way were sent a letter giving them the option of refusing to take part, and 652 postal refusals were received. The remaining names were forwarded to the fieldwork agency, who were set a target of 750 interviews. Because the sample was scattered geographically throughout Great Britain, it was not feasible within cost constraints to randomly select the required number of interviews from the pool, and each interviewer was allocated a quota based on region and sex to achieve from a larger number of addresses. The target of 750 was in fact overshot and 785 usable interviews were obtained.

As a quota sample, the concept of a response rate does not properly apply to this sample. However it is possible to check how representative it was of the original list of 2,710 trainees, by comparing the registration data for the two groups. On the whole those who were interviewed were reasonably representative of the wider pool, with significant differences on only a few variables. Women and older trainees were over-represented, and black women under-represented. Among the regions, London and to a lesser extent the West Midlands were under-represented, and the South East was over-represented for women but not for men. On planning group and course level the match between those who were interviewed and those who were not was quite close.

In order to correct for these biases , weights were calculated based on the joint distribution of age, sex and region in the original sample of 2,710 trainees and in the interview sample. These weights have been generally applied in the analysis (with the exception of Chapter Seven and the statistical models), and using them means that we can treat proportions derived from the interview sample as population estimates for all 1985/86 trainees. Unfortunately we were unable to correct for any bias resulting from differential geographical mobility. We did not have the resources to trace individuals who had moved from the address known to area offices, and the interview sample was necessarily biased against those who moved house to find work. As a result the study may underestimate the proportion of trainees who found work, particularly in the case of trainees at technological level or above, for whom there was indirect evidence of greater geographical mobility.

Once the interviews with trainees had been completed, it was possible to compare the information which trainees gave about themselves with the information supplied about them by area offices. This analysis showed that a number of people had been included in the sample who should not have been. The biggest group of errors concerned trainees who had left their course without completing it (an estimated 9.2 per cent of interviewees). The clustering of such errors within area offices (33 per cent of area offices accounted for 83 per cent of them, and 18 per cent of offices accounted for 63 per cent) suggested that they were due either to faulty administrative records or to a failure on the part of area offices to carry out the sampling instructions correctly, rather than to errors of recall on the part of respondents or errors of recording on the part of interviewers. Fortunately such errors were fairly evenly distributed across the 11 subject areas of training. Early leavers have generally been excluded from the analyses.

During the week beginning February 20 1989, more than two years after the end of their course, a postal questionnaire was sent to all 785 trainees who had been interviewed in the autumn of 1987. Despite the fact that the address list was 18 months old and that response rates are generally low in postal surveys, this brought in (after reminders) a total of 536 completed questionnaires, representing 68 per cent of the original interviewees. Given that trainees were seeking new jobs and as a result were more likely to move house than the population as a whole, this was a very respectable achievement.

Not surprisingly, response bias in the postal follow-up was bigger than in the original interview survey. Men, under-35s, members of ethnic minorities, those who trained in Greater London, in technological and manual fields, on operative level courses and on courses at technician level or higher were all under-represented. It was possible to make some allowance for these biases by adjusting specific estimates where there was relevant information in the interview survey.

The Comparison Sample

The matching process for the comparison sample dictated that fieldwork had to be carried out in two stages. The first stage involved a brief screening interview with a large number of people in order to locate people with the required characteristics. The second stage involved full scale interviews with selected individuals. This interview was designed to collect complete employment histories from 1980 onwards plus classifying information that was as comparable as possible to the information available for trainees. Screening was conducted via a commercial 'omnibus' survey, run by the same fieldwork agency that conducted the trainee interviews. This omnibus survey interviews a new random sample of 2,400 adults throughout Great Britain each week, using the electoral register as the sampling frame. Interviews are conducted face-to-face in the home, and last about 25 minutes. Response rates average around 50 per cent.

Information collected for screening purposes included age, sex, region of residence, occupation of head of household, economic activity status of respondents during 1986, and, for those who had been unemployed at any time during the year, the number and length of the spells of unemployment. Women who had been economically inactive in 1986 were also asked whether they had been looking for work, and women who had been employed part-time were asked whether they had been seeking full-time work. Before the matching process could be completed, the employment histories of trainees had first to be analysed. In consequence, while trainees were interviewed in the autumn of 1987, members of the comparison sample were not interviewed until the summer months of 1988.

The matching procedure was complex and entailed strict control over fieldwork procedures. We started by excluding from the total pool of names and addresses of people interviewed in the screening survey anyone who was aged under 18 or over 60 or who was in full-time education or training for any part of 1986. We then drew up a list of categories for matching, based partly on theoretical considerations and partly on the pragmatic issue of how many people were available in the pool in a given category. These categories were defined as follows:

For men:
- employed for the whole of 1986:
  - head of household
    - occupational classification (market research categories) by age by region
  - not head of household
    - age by region
- unemployed for part of 1986
  - starting date of unemployment spell by duration of employment spell by age

For women:
- employed full-time in 1986 (and never unemployed)
  - age by region
- employed part-time in 1986 (and never unemployed) but seeking full-time work at that time
  - age
- employed part-time in 1986 (and never unemployed) and not seeking full-time work at that time
  - age by region
- unemployed for part of 1986
  - starting date of unemployment spell by duration of employment spell by age
- economically inactive for all of 1986 but seeking work at that time
  - age

These categories gave a total of 185 different groups for matching. We then computed a table from the trainee data which told us how many individuals we needed to interview in each group in order to achieve a matched comparison sample of similar size, and uprated these numbers to allow for non-response. Next we randomly ordered the list of people in the full screening survey pool in order to get rid of any concealed bias in the list, and allocated people from the pool to each group on the basis of their characteristics. The people in each of the 185 groups were divided into two lists, the first containing the exact number of people that it was our target to interview in that group, the second being a reserve list to be used in case of non-response. Names from the reserve list were issued to interviewers only after four calls at an address had failed to produce an interview, and they were issued one at a time following the original random ordering. This was designed to minimise any response bias towards people who were more easily contactable. If all the names from the reserve list were exhausted, names were taken from the group which provided the next best match, for example an adjacent age group. The procedure for issuing substitutes was closely supervised, and meant that interviewing of the comparison sample, which started in June 1988, was not completed until October. In total, 760 usable interviews were obtained, each lasting on average around half an hour.

It proved much easier to obtain the target number of interviews in some groups than others. The biggest problem was finding women who were economically inactive throughout 1986 but were seeking work then. In order to match with women trainees who were economically inactive before starting their course we needed 105 names in this category, plus a margin for non-response, but screening yielded only 51. The shortfall was made up from women who had been economically inactive in 1986 without seeking work.

Figure A1.1 Percentages of men in trainee and comparison samples who were unemployed in each month from January 1980 until interview

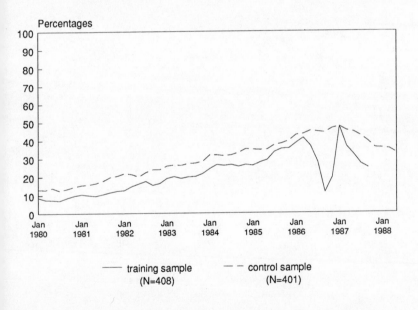

Source: Evaluation Study.

Note: Unweighted figures.

Crosstabulation of age by sex in the trainee and comparison samples showed that older men were over-represented in the latter, but that otherwise the correspondence was quite good.

Figure A1.1 plots the proportions of men in the trainee and comparison samples who were unemployed in each month from January 1980 up until the date of interview. For matching purposes we were concerned only with the period before training. In fact the unemployment rate for the comparison sample closely shadows the rate for trainees from 1980 right up until 1986. During this period the comparison group unemployment rate was consistently higher than the rate for trainees, but this was easily taken care of in the statistical models. The important point is that, prior to training, male trainees

Figure A1.2 Percentages of women in trainee and comparison samples who were in work in each month from January 1980 until interview

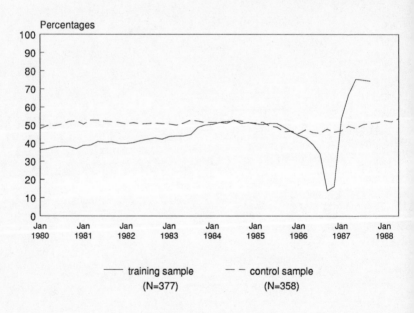

Source: Evaluation Study.

Note: Unweighted figures.

and non-trainees were set broadly on the same course. Men in the trainee and comparison samples were also well matched over the years 1980 to 1986 on the proportion in work and the proportion in full time education or training.

As explained above, matching proved more difficult for women, but it had some success. It was very good on the proportions in full-time education or training over the periods 1980-1986. However the match on the proportion in work (a more appropriate measure of labour market status for women than the unemployment rate) was more problematic. As Figure A1.2 shows, for women trainees this proportion rose gradually from 1980 to the end of 1983 and reached a plateau during 1984 and the first half of 1985. As they started their training courses the proportion in work fell, and then rose again steeply as the courses came to an end. The matching process was successful to the extent that during 1984 and 1985 the proportion of women in work in the comparison sample coincided very closely with the proportion in the training sample. However for the non-trainees this proportion had remained more or less constant between 1980 and 1984, whereas for the trainee sample it had risen steadily between these dates. This undoubtedly reflected differences between the two samples in long-term intentions regarding work. If we had confined the comparison between the two samples to the two years preceding training, we might have been very well satisfied with the closeness of the match.

The purpose of the matching was, of course, merely to reduce the variance between the trainee and comparison samples, and the differences described above were taken account of in the multivariate models testing the significance of the 'training effect' by the inclusion of measures of employment history among the predictor variables.

Appendix Two: Statistical Models

MODEL 1 Proportional hazards model for number of months before entry to the first job after the end of training

	mean	coefficient	t statistic
TTWA unemployment rate	13.52	-0.031**	-3.15
months unemployed immediately before course	8.03	-0.011***	-3.35
months in work since Jan. 1980	42.37	0.004*	2.49
female	0.49	0.424**	2.62
age	33.97	-0.016**	-2.83
ethnic minority	0.14	-0.340*	-2.52
disability/health problem	0.15	-0.244	-1.95
married	0.62	0.236	1.64
number of dependent children:			
0	0.46	..	..
1-2	0.40	-0.011	-0.08
3 or more	0.14	0.157	0.94
child aged under 5	0.04	-0.299	-1.36
lone parent	0.07	0.124	0.54
educational qualifications:			
none	0.22	..	..
below A Level standard	0.53	0.116	1.02
A Level standard or better	0.25	0.136	0.93
age left full-time education:			
16 or younger	0.67	..	..
17-19	0.23	0.265*	2.41
20 or older	0.10	0.195	1.19
trained in a new field	0.52	-0.117	-1.30
type of course:			
technological	0.19	..	..
clerical/secretarial	0.47	-0.279	-0.39
manual	0.34	0.056	0.08
level of course:			
skilled	0.76	..	..
technician or higher	0.19	-0.063	-0.09
operative	0.05	-0.217	-0.95

continued.../

	mean	coefficient	t statistic
location of course:			
college	0.43	..	..
private training institute	0.21	0.151	1.25
skill centre	0.36	0.077	0.49
length of course (months)	4.86	-0.011	-0.57
qualifications gained on course:			
none	0.38	..	..
unrecognised only	0.17	0.074	0.59
recognised	0.45	0.077	0.78

N:	702
N censored:	112
log-likelihood:	-3542
df:	26

Significance levels: *=.05, **=.01, ***=.001

MODEL 2 Proportional hazards model for number of months before entry to the first job after the end of training which used the skills learned

	mean	coefficient	t statistic
TTWA unemployment rate	13.52	-0.035**	-3.07
months unemployed immediately before course	8.03	-0.010**	-2.66
months in work since Jan. 1980	42.37	0.002	1.15
female	0.49	0.425*	2.21
age	33.97	-0.007	-1.02
ethnic minority	0.14	-0.120	-0.81
disability/health problem	0.15	-0.348*	-2.30
married	0.62	0.133	0.79
number of dependent children:			
0	0.46	..	..
1-2	0.40	0.018	0.11
3 or more	0.14	0.125	0.64
child aged under 5	0.04	-0.027	-0.12
lone parent	0.07	0.089	0.34
educational qualifications:			
none	0.22	..	..
below A Level standard	0.53	0.116	0.87
A Level standard or better	0.25	0.012	0.07
age left full-time education:			
16 or younger	0.67	..	..
17-19	0.23	0.354**	2.83
20 or older	0.10	0.273	1.45
trained in a new field	0.52	-0.111	-1.06
type of course:			
technological	0.19	..	..
clerical or commercial	0.47	0.146	0.14
manual	0.34	0.603	0.59
level of course:			
skilled	0.76	..	..
technician or higher	0.19	0.218	0.21
operative	0.05	-0.150	-0.56

continued.../

	mean	coefficient	t statistic
location of course:			
college	0.43	..	..
private training institute	0.21	0.210	1.52
skill centre	0.36	0.033	0.18
length of course (months)	4.86	0.028	1.32
qualifications gained on course:			
none	0.38	..	..
unrecognised only	0.17	0.129	0.88
recognised	0.45	0.280*	2.45

N:	702
N censored:	266
log-likelihood:	-2699
df:	26

Significance levels: *=.05, **=.01, ***=.001

MODEL 3   OLS regression model for the change in women's earnings after training

	mean	coefficient	t statistic
constant	..	264.90	..
earnings before course	299.17	-0.58***	3.53
TTWA unemployment rate	12.06	-3.32*	2.33
time away from work before course:			
in work before course	0.48	..	..
1-11 months	0.33	-1.66	0.12
12 months or more	0.19	8.34	0.50
last job before course:			
clerical & related	0.43	..	..
managerial/professional & rel.	0.15	-9.87	0.50
low skill service or manual	0.42	18.94	1.37
age	35.13	-0.82	0.93
ethnic minority	0.20	38.24*	2.39
disability/health problem	0.09	10.25	0.49
marital status:			
single	0.15	..	..
married	0.69	-1.30	0.06
widowed/separated/divorced	0.16	-18.43	0.74
number of dependent children:			
0	0.36	..	..
1-2	0.53	-14.08	0.89
3 or more	0.11	-44.62	1.89
child aged under 5	0.08	-212.90***	3.80
educational qualifications:			
below O Level standard/none	0.37	..	..
1-4 O Levels or equivalent	0.31	-0.70	0.05
5 O Levels or better	0.32	4.55	0.29
trained in a new field	0.47	-78.22**	2.59
type of course:			
clerical/secretarial	0.91	..	..
technological	0.04	73.32*	2.15
manual	0.05	-2.71	0.09

continued.../

	mean	coefficient	t statistic
qualifications gained on course:			
none	0.29	..	..
unrecognised only	0.15	4.60	0.25
recognised	0.56	-9.92	0.69
in job using skills ("in trade")	0.78	116.40*	2.44
Interaction terms:			
earnings before course with child under 5		0.80***	4.91
earnings before course with new kind of work		0.15	1.72
earnings before course with in trade		-0.38*	2.35

R Square	76.64
N	171
df	145

Significance levels: * =.05, ** =.01, *** =.001

Note: Dependent variable is the difference in actual gross hourly earnings in pence between the last job before training and the current or most recent job following training, both uprated to Oct. 1987 values.

MODEL 4 Logit model for employment in the period April 1987 – September 1987: combined trainee and comparison sample, women

	mean	exponentiated coefficient	t statistic
Constant	..	6.21	..
TTWA unemployment rate	13.26	0.99	0.40
months unemployed in 1985	1.77	0.97	1.28
months in work 1980-1985	40.63	1.01^{**}	2.80
Job (or latest job) in 1986:			
clerical & related	0.34	1.00	..
managerial/professional	0.18	0.98	0.06
personal service	0.34	1.14	0.48
manufacturing blue collar	0.13	0.71	1.02
other	0.01	1.78	0.60
age	35.50	0.96^{**}	3.08
ethnic minority	0.17	0.97	0.09
disability/health problem	0.12	0.54^{*}	2.10
married	0.72	1.18	0.42
number of dependent children:			
0	0.35	1.00	..
1-2	0.56	1.60	1.50
3 or more	0.09	2.83^{*}	2.08
child aged under 5	0.21	0.15^{***}	6.06
lone parent	0.12	1.15	0.28
educational qualifications:			
none	0.34	1.00	..
below A Level standard	0.47	1.11	0.41
A Level standard or better	0.19	0.79	0.64
age left full-time education:			
16 or younger	0.70	1.00	..
17-19	0.23	1.48	1.30
20 or older	0.07	2.26	1.55

continued.../

	mean	exponentiated coefficient	t statistic
months in full-time training or education 1980-1985	2.74	1.01	0.58
went on TOPS/OJTS	0.52	2.21**	3.12

N:	594
deviance:	593 (df 572)
deviance with constant only:	692 (df 593)

Significance levels: *=.05, **=.01, ***=.001

Note: Trainee sample excludes those whose course started before Jan. 1986 or ended after Mar. 1987, and those who had never worked before their course. Comparison sample excludes those with no job before July 1986.

MODEL 5 Logit model for employment in the period April 1987 - September 1987: combined trainee and comparison sample, men

	mean	exponentiated coefficient	t statistic
Constant	..	20.08	..
TTWA unemployment rate	14.56	0.95[*]	2.11
months unemployed in 1985	3.78	0.88[***]	4.93
months in work 1980-1985	47.57	1.02[**]	3.01
Job (or latest job) in 1986:			
manufacturing blue collar	0.38	1.00	
managerial/professional	0.15	3.21[**]	2.97
clerical & related	0.06	0.83	0.41
personal service	0.13	0.95	0.17
construction/mining/transport	0.22	1.09	0.32
other	0.06	0.79	0.57
age	33.41	0.94[***]	4.92
ethnic minority	0.13	0.47[*]	2.39
disability/health problem	0.14	0.55[*]	2.15
married	0.60	1.24	0.63
number of dependent children:			
0	0.55	1.00	..
1-2	0.32	1.16	0.43
3 or more	0.13	0.95	0.12
child aged under 5	0.25	0.58	1.71
lone parent	0.03	1.85	0.86
educational qualifications:			
none	0.32	1.00	..
below A Level standard	0.44	1.26	0.96
A Level or better	0.24	1.15	0.41
age left full-time education:			
16 or younger	0.79	1.00	..
17-19	0.13	2.25[*]	2.00
20 or older	0.08	0.82	0.45

continued...\/

	mean	exponentiated coefficient	t statistic
months in full-time training or education 1980-1985	3.68	1.03*	2.23
went on TOPS/OJTS	0.53	2.72***	4.38

N:	707
deviance:	609 (df 685)
deviance with constant only:	833 (df 706)

Significance levels: *=.05, **=.01, ***=.001

Note: Trainee sample excludes those whose course started before Jan. 1986 or ended after Mar. 1987 and those who had never worked before their course. Comparison sample excludes those with no job before July 1986.

MODEL 6 Logit model for job satisfaction in current job: combined trainee and comparison sample, women

	mean	exponentiated coefficient	t statistic
constant	..	0.41	..
TTWA unemployment rate	13.04	0.98	0.94
months unemployed in 1985	1.44	1.00	0.13
months in work 1980-1985	42.39	1.01	1.51
job (or latest job) in 1986:			
clerical & related	0.36	1.00	..
managerial/professional & rel.	0.16	1.69	1.42
personal service	0.37	1.37	1.13
manufacturing blue collar	0.09	1.48	0.86
other	0.02	1.46	0.51
age	35.71	0.97	1.80
ethnic minority	0.17	0.55	1.84
disability/health problem	0.09	0.68	0.92
married	0.72	6.07***	3.92
number of dependent children:			
0	0.36	1.00	..
1-2	0.55	0.40**	2.72
3 or more	0.09	0.27*	2.56
child aged under 5	0.14	1.27	0.62
lone parent	0.11	4.52**	2.58
educational qualifications:			
none	0.31	1.00	..
below A Level standard	0.51	1.58	1.59
A Level standard or better	0.18	1.31	0.62
age left full-time education:			
16 or younger	0.67	1.00	..
17-19	0.27	1.00	0.01
20 or older	0.06	0.26*	2.09
months in full-time training or education 1980-1985	2.56	1.01	0.82

continued.../

	mean	exponentiated coefficient	t statistic
training:			
none (comparison sample)	0.43	1.00	..
TOPS/OJTS, working out of trade	0.12	1.79	1.43
TOPS/OJTS, working in trade	0.45	2.32**	2.84

N:	382	
deviance:	474	(df 359)
deviance with constant only:	519	(df 381)

Significance levels: *=.05, **=.01, ***=.001

Note: Excludes trainees who had never worked before their course and members of the comparison sample with no job before July 1986. Both samples exclude respondents who were not in work at the time of interview.

MODEL 7 Logit model for job satisfaction in current job: combined trainee and comparison sample, men

	mean	exponentiated coefficient	t statistic
constant	..	0.74	..
TTWA unemployment rate	14.09	0.99	0.48
months unemployed in 1985	2.71	0.99	0.22
months in work 1980-1985	51.88	1.00	0.58
job (or latest job) in 1986:			
clerical & related	0.06	1.00	..
managerial/professional & rel.	0.18	1.14	0.26
personal service	0.14	0.99	0.01
manufacturing blue collar	0.35	1.03	0.07
other	0.27	0.72	0.67
age	32.57	0.98	1.28
ethnic minority	0.12	0.71	1.04
disability/health problem	0.10	1.57	1.30
married	0.59	1.52	1.21
number of dependent children:			
0	0.56	1.00	..
1-2	0.32	1.07	0.20
3 or more	0.12	0.67	0.87
child aged under 5	0.23	1.38	0.94
lone parent	0.03	4.60[*]	2.19
educational qualifications:			
none	0.27	1.00	..
below A Level standard	0.47	0.45[**]	2.90
A Level standard or better	0.26	0.64	1.35
age left full-time education:			
16 or younger	0.78	1.00	..
17-19	0.15	1.44	1.16
20 or older	0.07	1.01	0.02
months in full-time training or education 1980-1985	4.12	1.01	0.84

continued.../

181

	mean	exponentiated coefficient	t statistic
training:			
none (comparison sample)	0.47	1.00	..
TOPS/OJTS, working out of trade	0.18	1.01	0.04
TOPS/OJTS, working in trade	0.35	3.52***	4.83

N:	458
deviance:	556 (df 435)
deviance with constant only:	607 (df 457)

Significance levels: *=.05, **=.01, ***=.001

Note: Excludes trainees who had never worked before their course and members of the comparison sample with no job before July 1986. Both samples exclude respondents who were not in work at the time of interview.

MODEL 8 OLS regression model for earnings: combined trainee and control sample, women

	mean	coefficient	t statistic
Constant	..	300.20	..
TTWA unemployment rate	13.02	-2.54	1.88
months unemployed in 1985	1.61	-3.37*	2.08
months in work 1980-85	41.29	0.81*	2.07
Job (or latest job) in 1986:			
clerical & related	0.36	..	..
managerial/professional & rel.	0.16	42.09*	2.24
personal service	0.35	-18.46	1.33
manufacturing blue collar	0.12	-6.65	0.33
construction/mining/transport	0.01	-61.77	0.99
other	0.01	-37.19	0.49
age group:			
18-25	0.14	..	..
25-34	0.31	-29.81	1.29
35-44	0.42	-35.24	1.45
45+	0.13	-38.17	1.41
ethnic minority	0.17	25.13	1.63
disability/health problem	0.08	-11.84	0.58
married	0.71	8.60	0.42
number of dependent children:			
none	0.35	..	..
1-2	0.55	-0.89	0.05
3 or more	0.10	-10.51	0.40
child aged under 5	0.15	-8.71	0.46
lone parent	0.12	-0.08	0.00
educational qualifications:			
none	0.31	..	..
below A Level standard	0.50	23.76***	1.19
A level standard or better	0.19	155.00***	5.51
age left full-time education:			
16 or younger	0.67	..	..
17-19	0.26	19.38	1.28
20 or older	0.07	47.69	1.81

continued.../

	mean	coefficient	t statistic
months in full-time training or education 1980-1985	2.67	-0.61	0.81
training:			
none (comparison sample)	0.42	..	..
TOPS/OJTS, working out of trade	0.13	17.87	0.38
TOPS/OJTS, working in trade	0.45	82.52**	2.61
Interaction terms:			
months in work 1980-85 with trainee working out of trade		-0.02	0.03
months in work 1980-85 with trainee working in trade		-0.76	1.55
below A Lev, trainee working out of trade		-4.49	0.11
below A Lev, trainee working in trade		-20.86	0.70
A Lev+, trainee working out of trade		-200.10***	3.76
A Lev+, trainee working in trade		-141.50***	3.82

R Square   29.99%
N   377
df   345

Significance levels: *=.05, **=.01, ***=.001

Note: Excludes trainees who had never worked before their course and members of the comparison sample with no job before July 1986.

MODEL 9 OLS regression model for earnings: combined trainee and comparison sample, men

	mean	coefficient	t statistic
Constant	..	374.30	..
TTWA unemployment rate	14.64	-6.64***	3.72
months unemployed in 1985	3.04	-3.72	1.68
months in work 1980-85	49.02	1.35**	2.79
Job (or latest job) in 1986:			
manufacturing blue collar	0.39	..	..
managerial/professional & rel.	0.16	42.09	1.73
clerical & related	0.07	-13.15	0.42
personal service	0.13	-66.37**	2.75
construction/mining/transport	0.20	-38.91	1.86
other	0.06	-37.72	1.15
age group:			
18-25	0.29	..	..
25-34	0.38	-4.49	0.12
35-44	0.21	81.40	1.84
45+	0.11	83.07	1.68
ethnic minority	0.12	-13.64	0.56
disability/health problem	0.11	-46.24	1.94
married (or living as)	0.57	44.27	1.81
number of dependent children:			
0	0.57	..	..
1-2	0.31	-8.46	0.32
3 or more	0.12	-28.16	0.80
child aged under 5	0.22	19.82	0.79
lone parent	0.04	62.82	1.33
educational qualifications:			
none	0.27	..	..
below A Level standard	0.45	20.52	0.81
A level standard or better	0.28	129.40***	3.79
age left full-time education:			
16 or younger	0.74	..	..
17-19	0.18	18.43	0.85
20 or older	0.08	38.75	1.19

continued.../

	mean	coefficient	t statistic
months in full-time training or education 1980-1985	4.65	0.40	0.42
training:			
no training (comparison sample)	0.44	..	..
TOPS/OJTS, working out of trade	0.22	6.12**	0.11
TOPS/OJTS, working in trade	0.34	138.60**	2.73
Interaction terms:			
age 25-34, trainee working out of trade		-26.48	0.52
age 25-34, trainee working in trade		-47.26	0.98
age 35-44, trainee working out of trade		-62.02*	1.02
age 35-44, trainee working in trade		-133.7*	2.45
age 45+, trainee working out of trade		-182.6*	2.51
age 45+, trainee working in trade		-114.5*	1.79
below A Lev, trainee working out of trade		55.23	1.33
below A Lev, trainee working in trade		-71.67	1.70
A Lev+, trainee working out of trade		-32.99	0.60
A Lev+, trainee working in trade		-169.40***	3.55

$$R \text{ Square} \quad 31.56\%$$
$$N \quad 409$$
$$df \quad 373$$

Significance levels: *=.05, **=.01, ***=.001

Note: Excludes trainees who had never worked before their course and members of the comparison sample with no job before July 1986.

References

Berthoud, R. (1978) *Training Adults for Skilled Jobs: Skill Centre Training and Local Labour Markets*. London: Policy Studies Institute Vol. XLIV No. 575.

Brown, C. (1984) *Black and White Britain: The Third PSI Survey*. London: PSI and Heinemann.

Cockburn, C. (1987) *Two-Track Training: Sex Inequalities and the YTS*. Basingstoke and London: Macmillan Education.

Clarke, K., (forthcoming, 1991) *Women and Training: A Review of Recent Research and Policy*. Manchester: Equal Opportunities Commission.

Confederation of British Industry (1989) *Towards a Skills Revolution: Report of the Vocational Education and Training Task Force*. London: CBI.

Coyle, A. (1982) 'Sex and Skill in the Organisation of the Clothing Industry', in J. West (ed.), *Work, Women and the Labour Market*. London: Routledge and Kegan Paul.

Department of Education and Science (1988) *English School Leavers 1986-87*. Statistical Bulletin 13/88.

Department of Education and Science (1990) *International Statistical Comparisons of the Education and Training of 16 to 18 year olds*. Statistical Bulletin 1/90.

de Sousa, E. (1989) 'YTS – The Racism Riddle'. *Unemployment Bulletin*, No. 29, Spring, pp 23-24.

Dunne, P. and Elias, P. (1986) *Jobs After TOPS: An Analysis of Survey Data from the Training Opportunities Scheme*. Coventry: University of Warwick, Institute for Employment Research.

Employment Department (1988) *Employment for the 1990s*. London: HMSO.

Employment Department (1990a) "ET Follow-up Survey of Scheme Leavers". *Labour Market Quarterly Report*, November, pp 16-18.

Employment Department (1990b) *1990s: The Skills Decade. Strategic Guidance on Enterprise and Training*. Sheffield.

Green, F. (1991) 'Sex discrimination in Job-Related Training'. *British Journal of Industrial Relations*, Vol. 29, pp 295-304.

Hakim, C. (1979) *Occupational Segregation*. London: Department of Employment Research Paper No. 9.

House of Commons Expenditure Committee (1973) *The Employment of Women: Sixth Report*. London: HMSO.

Institute for Employment Research (1989a) *Review of the Economy and Employment 1989*. Coventry: University of Warwick.

Institute for Employment Research (1989b) *Review of the Economy and Employment: Occupational Assessment*. Coventry: University of Warwick.

Joshi, H. (1984) *Women's Participation in Paid Work: Further Analysis of the Women and Employment Survey*. London: Department of Employment Research Paper No. 45.

König, W. (1987) 'Employment and Career Mobility of Women in France and the Federal Republic', in W. Teckenberg (ed.), *Comparative Studies of Social Structure: Recent Research on France, the US, and the Federal Republic of Germany*. Armonk, N.Y. and London: M.E. Sharpe.

LaLonde, R. (1986) 'Evaluating the Econometric Evaluations of Training Programs with Experimental Data'. *American Economic Review*, Vol. 76.

Lee, D., Marsden, D., Rickman, P. and Duncombe, J. (1990) *Scheming for Youth: A Study of YTS in the Enterprise Culture*. Buckingham: Open University Press.

McLeish, H. (1990) 'Who Pays for Skills?' *Labour Market Briefing* No. 3. London: House of Commons.

McRae, S. (1991 forthcoming) *Maternity Rights in Britain*. London: Policy Studies Institute.

Manpower Services Commission (1972) *Classification of Occupations and Directory of Occupational Titles* (3 Vols. with later Supplements). London: HMSO.

Martin, J. and Roberts, C. (1984) *Women and Employment: A Lifetime Perspective.* Department of Employment and OPCS, London: HMSO.

Metcalf, H. and Leighton, P. (1989) *The Under-Utilisation of Women in the Labour Market.* London: Institute of Manpower Studies Report No. 172.

National Institute of Economic and Social Research (1989) *Productivity, Education and Training: Britain and Other Countries Compared.* London.

O'Connell, B. 1990 'Training Infrastructure – the Industry Level'. *Employment Gazette* Vol. 98 No. 7, pp 353-9.

OPCS Social Survey Division (1987) *General Household Survey 1985.* London: HMSO.

OPCS Social Survey Division (1989) *General Household Survey 1986.* London: HMSO.

OPCS Social Survey Division (1990) *General Household Survey 1988,* by K. Foster, A. Wilmot and J. Dobbs. London: HMSO.

Payne, J. (1989) *Adult Off-the-Job Skills Training: First Report to the Training Agency.* Sheffield: Training Agency.

Payne, J. (1990) *Adult Off-the-Job Skills Training: An Evaluation Study.* Sheffield: Training Agency Research and Development Series No. 57.

Prais, S. (1989) 'How Europe Would See the New British Initiative for Standardising Vocational Qualifications', Chapter 15 in National Institute of Economic and Social Research: *Productivity, Education and Training: Britain and Other Countries Compared.* London.

Rothwell, S. (1980) 'The United Kingdom', Chapter 5 in A.M. Yohalem (ed.), *Women Returning to Work: Policies and Progress in Five Countries.* London: Frances Pinter (Publishers) Ltd.

189

Shaw, L.B. (1983) 'Problems of Labor Market Re-entry', Chapter 2 in L.B. Shaw (ed.): *Unplanned Careers: The Working Lives of Middle-Aged Women.* Lexington, USA: Lexington Books.

Sheldrake, J. and Vickerstaff, S. (1987) *The History of Industrial Training in Britain.* Aldershot: Avebury (Gower Publishing Co. Ltd.)

Smith, E. (1990) *Skill Needs in Britain 1990.* London: IFF Research Ltd.

Unemployment Unit and Youthaid (1990) 'ET: The Real Results'. *Working Brief* November, pp 1-2.

Unemployment Unit and Youthaid (1991) 'ET: The Manchester TEC'. *Working Brief* January, p 3.

Wickham, A. (1986) *Women and Training.* Milton Keynes: Open University Press *Gender and Education* Series.

Wilson, J. (1990) 'High Technology National Training'. *Employment Gazette* Vol. 98 No. 7, pp 347-52.